BY FAITH

STRENGTH AND HOPE FOR LIFE'S CHALLENGES

CHRIS MORRIS

Our Daily Bread
Publishing®

Published in association with Books & Such Literary Management, 52 Mission Circle, Suite 122, PMB 170, Santa Rosa, CA 95409-5370, www.booksandsuch.com.

Requests for permission to quote from this book should be directed to: Permissions Department, Our Daily Bread Publishing, PO Box 3566, Grand Rapids, MI 49501, or contact us by email at permissionsdept@odb.org.

Scripture quotations, unless otherwise indicated, are taken from the Holy Bible, New Living Translation, copyright © 1996, 2004, 2015 by Tyndale House Foundation. Used by permission of Tyndale House Publishers, Inc., Carol Stream, Illinois 60188. All rights reserved.

Scripture quotations marked NIV are taken from the Holy Bible, New International Version®, NIV®. Copyright © 1973, 1978, 1984, 2011 by Biblica, Inc.™ Used by permission of Zondervan. All rights reserved worldwide. www.zondervan.com.

Interior design by Michael J. Williams

Library of Congress Cataloging-in-Publication Data Available

Printed in the United States of America
24 25 26 27 28 29 30 31 / 8 7 6 5 4 3 2 1

For Barbara, who believed in me before anyone else

CONTENTS

INTRODUCTION

Life is hard, isn't it? There's no escaping that simple fact. Whether it's a literal tornado bringing our house flat in a single moment or a metaphorical tornado bringing wreckage into our lives relationally, some days are just rough. If we're really honest with ourselves, sometimes we can't help but wonder if God is paying attention to everything that goes awry. We know in our heads that the Bible says He loves us and cares deeply for us, but if that's the case why is everything so hard? The book of Hebrews speaks directly to these challenges by showing us the value of perseverance when the promises of God seem distant.

This question of suffering has bothered saints through the ages. We're not going to fully solve that in a few pages here, but we can make some headway. The first thing we must remember is that this world is busted. Ever since Adam and Eve took a bite of that fruit, everything has been sideways. Life has been hard for men and women, and the book of Romans tells us that even creation is groaning anxiously, awaiting its redemption. *Everything* is askew. Nothing works the way it's supposed to work. This affects every moment of every day, with no exceptions.

But there's more to the equation than simply saying the world isn't functioning the way God initially intended.

There's also a false narrative about how the Christian life is supposed to work. Too many people have said for too long that a mature Christian life should be blessed. They're not wrong about having blessings from God, but things get a little sketchy when we start thinking about what it looks like to be blessed by God. A lot of people say or insinuate that a blessed life means one without problems, and they may even go further to say that if there are problems, it's an indication of a lack of maturity in our lives. This just isn't true.

The biblical stories in the Old and New Testaments don't reflect this idea. Abraham had all sorts of problems in his life—he had to separate from his cousin Lot because their workers were arguing with one another, he went to war with five ancient kings to rescue Lot, he was promised a son but didn't have one until he was one hundred years old, and the list goes on. Maybe you've felt like you're at war with others for the sake of righteousness, and it doesn't make any sense to you.

Job had all kinds of calamities hit his life, and the reason is fascinating. In somewhat of a cosmic bet between God and Satan, Satan says that Job lives a blameless life only because he is wealthy and happy. God gives Satan permission to bring all kinds of destruction into Job's life, specifically to *prove* that Job is a faithful man because of his heart, not because of his material blessings. Job literally loses all his wealth and his children in a single day, and he didn't do a thing to bring it on himself. Maybe you're going through a season of terrible loss and find yourself confused.

David was called a man after God's own heart in the Scriptures, and God made an eternal covenant with David's family because of his love for David. Yet David had an incredibly dysfunctional family, largely because of the consequences of his own sin against—his sexual exploitation of—Bathsheba (2 Samuel 12:7–12). Years later, one of his sons slept with David's concubines and bragged about it publicly. Another started a rebellion and kicked David out of Jerusalem. One of his daughters was raped by one of his sons. Maybe you have dysfunction in your own family and find yourself overwhelmed by it.

Jesus promised we would have troubles. In John 16:33 He says, "Here on earth you will have many trials and sorrows. But take heart, because I have overcome the world." This is the paradigm that we need to understand to gain better insight into the consequences of trials, sins, accidents, and calamities in our lives. There is no such thing as a trouble-free life on this planet. Everyone inherits problems. But what does Jesus mean when He says He has overcome the world?

Jesus means a couple of things, and both are relevant for us today. First, He means that He is eventually going to right everything that's been wrong about this world. A day is coming where everything that's upside down is going to be put right side up—all the pain is going to fade, all the disappointments are going to disappear, and all the confusion is going to go away. There is a new world coming, and in this world, everything will make sense. Jesus will be rightly crowned as king of this new world, and He will rule with perfect justice. We'll no longer have the frustrations of loss and sorrow that we deal with every day, because the world will eventually be set right. This is a great reason for hope, and this hope for a new world can quench that desire we all have for things to make sense in this world. But there's more to comprehend about Jesus overcoming the world.

The key to the second aspect of Jesus overcoming the world is found in one of the stories of His resurrection. Jesus lets Thomas touch the scars on His side and His hands so that Thomas would believe that Jesus was truly resurrected. Often this story is pointed to negatively, as though Thomas should have been able to easily believe that someone would rise from the dead. Like it's a normal occurrence. Even if I had seen Jesus raise several people from the grave as Thomas had, I know I'd still want to see the scars too. Let's think a little more about those scars, though.

Jesus was in His resurrected body, His perfect body after death, and yet He had scars from His death on the cross that Thomas could touch. We'd think that a resurrected body would be a perfect body, but it's not, at least not for Jesus. No, Jesus had the scars from His terrible, bloody, violent death still on His body; I'd guess He had other scars from His life too. The scars of Jesus can speak powerfully to us about how God views things that happen in our life.

God could have removed the scars from Jesus's body. He could have erased any effects of that terrible event from the body of Jesus so that Jesus wouldn't have to remember being stabbed by a spear every time He looked down at His abdomen. He could have removed the scars from the hands of Jesus, so He wouldn't have to remember the excruciating pain of being nailed to a cross when He was entirely innocent. But God didn't do this. He left the scars on the body of Jesus. Even though they no longer cause pain, they are reminders of past events.

So it is in our lives. God is always looking to stir faith in our lives, even through difficult times. Perhaps especially through difficult times. God reminds us of the challenges we suffered through. He leaves the scars from our past on our bodies, in our minds, and upon our souls. This is not because He's a vindictive God or because He enjoys causing pain in those He loves, but because there is always beauty to be found in hard times. C. S. Lewis said in *The Problem of Pain*, "God whispers to us in our pleasures, speaks in our conscience, but shouts in our pains: it is his megaphone to rouse a deaf world." To extend the metaphor a bit, this megaphone echoes, and we can remember the lessons we've learned through our hard times by revisiting our sorrows. It can stir our faith.

I've written this devotional to remind us of what it looks like to examine the hard times in our lives for the evidence of God's goodness, His faithfulness, and His presence.

On this forty-day journey, you will travel through the "Hall of Faith" found in Hebrews 11 and consider the nature of faith in dark times. You'll get to experience the stories of most of the faithful individuals who are featured in Hebrews 11—men and women such as Abraham and Sarah, Jochebed and Amram, David, and Rahab. No matter their setbacks or hardships, their diverse backgrounds or upbringings, their individual failings or victories, these men and women will help give you a vision for standing on the promises of God.

You'll begin each reading by inviting God to participate in your devotional time. Then you'll focus your thoughts on one or two verses. Inspired by these verses, you'll be challenged to seek God during seasons of struggle or hardship and will be encouraged to push toward God instead of pulling back. Toward the end of each reading is an opportunity to journal in response to the truths discussed, followed by a meditative prayer. Each reading ends with a blessing to help strengthen and encourage you to seek God's presence, nearness, and love in hard times.

May this devotional inspire you to draw near to God, whether you are in a season of discouragement or inspiration. May you find the presence of God in new and exciting places in your life over the next forty days. May your heart be strengthened and your mind renewed as you ponder these characters of the Bible in new ways.

1

FAITH DEFINED

Faith shows the reality of what we hope for;
it is the evidence of things we cannot see.

HEBREWS 11:1

*Dear Jesus, teach me what it means to have faith,
especially when I can't see where I'm placing my hope.*

Whatever is good and perfect is a gift coming down to
us from God our Father, who created all the lights in the
heavens. He never changes or casts a shifting shadow.

JAMES 1:17

Faith is a difficult thing to grab hold of because it's not tangible. We can't touch it, feel it, or see it in any way. And it becomes even more difficult when we are trying to put our faith in Jesus, because He is someone we've never physically met. Instead, we are putting our trust in a person who lived on this earth some two thousand years ago, believing that He truly loves us, despite having no physical interaction with Him.

Even worse, sometimes life seems to tell us that Jesus doesn't want to be all that involved in our lives. Divorce breaks up families, sickness and death destroy relationships, and depression and anxiety wait in the wings to wreck what's left of hope. Just where is He amid all this sorrow? What reason do we have to cling to faith when

Jesus seems at best disinterested in fixing anything that's going on in our lives?

As strange as it sounds, this heartache is the very birthplace of faith. Faith isn't something that makes logical sense, because it's not based on the scientific method. It can't be tested or proven or shown to be accurate through investigation. No, faith is something we must choose based on what we haven't seen. Faith is that thing we hold tight to when nothing makes sense. How do we develop faith if it's not based on rational thought? How can we begin to believe in something we haven't seen firsthand?

This is a bit of a trick question because, whether or not we have recognized them, each of us has seen the fingerprints of God in our lives. Remember, every good and perfect gift comes from the Father of lights. What a powerful thought! *Every good thing* that comes into our lives is a gift from God. That promotion you weren't expecting—God demonstrating His love for you. That parking spot right in the front of the mall—God taking care of even the little things in your life. That moment with your teenager when you finally connected with her heart after what felt like years of distance—God showing up to remind you that He is for you.

The way to develop faith, then, is to recognize what God is already doing. Once you gain some vision for the way He is already interacting with your life, you will begin to build a personal history of His faithfulness. Much like a book of answered prayers would help us see that God hears us, this reassessment of all good things as coming from God can build your faith, because you will see that He is never silent or unmoved by the circumstances in your life.

On the lines below, write down at least five ways that the Father of lights has shown Himself to be a giver of good gifts in your life in the last month. Be as creative as you need to be—it might be that you're in a tough season and you need to thank Him for your breath. It still counts.

_____

_____

_____

_____

_____

_____

_____

_____

_____

_____

_____

_____

_____

_____

_____

_____

_____

_____

_____

_____

_____

_____

_____

_____

*Jesus, give me eyes to see the places where
You've intervened in my life. Help me to see
that You are always with me, even when times
are dark. Remind me of Your unending love
for me when I'm walking through dark times,
and remind me to celebrate Your good gifts
every time I stumble across them. Amen.*

BLESSING

May you have fresh eyes to see the tender care of God in
your everyday life. May you be forever changed, day by
day, as you begin to see the activity of God in the normal
moments. May you remember that Jesus can use ordinary occurrences as well as supernatural ones to show
His attentive care for you.

2

THE FAITH OF OUR ANCESTORS

Through their faith, the people in days
of old earned a good reputation.

HEBREWS 11:2

*Dear Jesus, help me understand how the patriarchs and
matriarchs found faith so that I can learn from them.*

Abraham never wavered in believing God's promise.
In fact, his faith grew stronger, and in this he brought
glory to God. He was fully convinced that God is
able to do whatever he promises. And because of
Abraham's faith, God counted him as righteous.

ROMANS 4:20–22

Abraham is a fascinating character study in faith.
God told Abraham when he was very old that he
would have a son (Genesis 17:15–27). Beyond that, God
told Abraham he would be the father of many nations. All
the while, he and his wife, Sarah, were quite old and past
the normal childbearing age. Both Abraham and Sarah
laughed at the idea of having a child at such an obviously
old age, but God was faithful anyway.

This is a vital point for us to hang on to for a moment or two. Because having a child at their advanced
ages didn't make sense to them naturally, both Abraham

19

and Sarah initially could do nothing but laugh at the idea of God fulfilling this particular promise to them. While God did confront Sarah for laughing, it doesn't appear that He judged either Abraham or Sarah for their laughter, because the promise wasn't based on them starting in a place of faith. It is the same with us: our journey can begin in disbelief or even laughter, and we will not earn judgment from God.

We see in Romans that Abraham grew strong in his faith over time. We all must start somewhere, and God is gracious in His dealings with us. By the time Abraham was promised a son, he already had a history with God. Because God had called Abraham to a land he would show him, Abraham had left his home and most of his family in Haran. Before any other promises were given, Abraham was called to leave the familiar and to trust God. Abraham left and felt the presence of God leading him eventually to Canaan. Over time, it became clear that God was giving Canaan to Abraham. Only after the promise of land did the promise of a son come. Even after these touches from God, the promise of a son was a difficult promise to believe because of biological realities. But it's obvious Abraham didn't stay in a place of mocking God's promise. Instead, he looked at his history with God and realized God is faithful and worth believing, even for the impossible.

We can do the same as Abraham and, indeed, this is exactly what we are called to do. While God's promise to Abraham was part of His specific plan of salvation, God still moves and speaks today. Like Abraham, we can look at the promises God has fulfilled and take courage from the fact that He is active in our lives. We can trust that God will continue to be faithful to us in our present and future, just as He has been in our past. But, and this is important, we can also have grace with ourselves when we find ourselves laughing at the absurdity of a promise from God. God will have grace with us as we grow into our faith, especially with the seemingly impossible promises. We should do the same with ourselves.

Think over your life and answer the following question: When has God proven His promises to be true in your life? If you feel stuck, look up some of God's promises to believers to prime the pump for this exercise. We can be certain there are fulfilled promises from God in our lives because He is faithful.

_____

_____

_____

_____

_____

_____

_____

_____

_____

_____

_____

_____

_____

_____

_____

_____

_____

_____

_____

_____

_____

*Jesus, thank You that You don't judge me
when I laugh at Your promises in my life.
Thank You for being generous with me when
I struggle to trust in You, Your love, and Your
goodness. Thank You for demonstrating Your
love to me in many practical ways. There is
no way I can doubt You are for me. Amen.*

BLESSING

May you grow in your faith as you consider the faithfulness of God in your life. May you have as much grace with yourself as God has with you. May you know that God sees you with eyes of approval.

3

CREATION CAN BUILD OUR FAITH

By faith we understand that the entire universe was
formed at God's command, that what we now see
did not come from anything that can be seen.

HEBREWS 11:3

*Dear Jesus, guide me into understanding
so that I can know what God creating
the world has to do with my faith.*

Christ is the visible image of the invisible God. He
existed before anything was created and is supreme
over all creation, for through him God created
everything in the heavenly realms and on earth.
He made the things we can see and the things we
can't see—such as thrones, kingdoms, rulers, and
authorities in the unseen world. Everything was
created through him and for him. He existed before
anything else, and he holds all creation together.

COLOSSIANS 1:15–17

We don't always think about God being the creator
of the universe, and there's a good reason for that. It
sometimes feels unrelated to anything relevant to our faith
today. What does it matter if God created the universe out
of nothing, or if some other force was behind the develop-
ment of the world as we know it?

Actually, it's surprisingly relevant to our faith that God is the creator. He is the only one who has ever created something from nothing. Think about that fact for just a moment. God didn't just create apples and giraffes and flowers, but He created the very idea of apples and giraffes and flowers. Before He came up with these ideas, nothing existed. It was all up to God to come up with everything that is in nature and existence.

But there's more at play here when we consider what Colossians says about Jesus. Colossians says that everything is held together by and through and for Jesus (Colossians 1:15–17). In other words, Jesus is still doing the job of holding everything in place. Without Jesus, gravity would be a part-time experience instead of always working. Without Jesus, sometimes a banana peel would hold a banana, and sometimes it would hold empty air. Without Jesus, the water cycle wouldn't be a thing and the oceans would dry up. Without Jesus, photosynthesis would be broken, and we wouldn't even be able to breathe.

Everything in nature points to the faithfulness of God working through Jesus. The fact that sunsets continue to happen day after day, that the moon is always in the sky, that leopards really don't change their spots—all these events point to the faithfulness of God. God remains intimately involved in all the minute details of creation, making sure that everything works just the way it's supposed to work. There are no places on Earth where an orange doesn't taste like an orange, or the wind doesn't uplift objects from the ground. Everything works just as it ought to work. Every day. Without fail.

This can and should stir up faith in our spirits. We can see the faithfulness of God in all the intricacies of the earth, as created by its Creator. We can glimpse the consistency of God by viewing nature. We can draw on His ability to always be on the job with the natural world as proof that He won't let us down in our lives. Even when things seem awry, we can trust God because He is the very definition of faithful. Nature proves it.

Consider all the different aspects of nature and pick your favorite. Maybe it's the way water flows down Multnomah Falls in the Pacific Northwest, or how you never see the same sunset twice. What does this element of nature say about the faithfulness of God? As you meditate on God's consistency, take time to rest in the assurance of His faithfulness to you.

_____

_____

_____

_____

_____

_____

_____

_____

_____

_____

*Jesus, I confess I haven't considered
Your faithfulness and consistency in my
life enough. Instead, I've taken it for
granted that You hold everything up by
the power of Your word. Teach me to
look for Your hand in all things. Amen.*

BLESSING

May you see the faithfulness of God surrounding you in
your daily life. May you walk in the wisdom of His consistency as demonstrated in nature. May you see the work
of God in fresh ways and be drawn into deeper faith.

4

ABEL GAVE
A BETTER OFFERING

It was by faith that Abel brought a more acceptable
offering to God than Cain did. Abel's offering gave
evidence that he was a righteous man, and God
showed his approval of his gifts. Although Abel is long
dead, he still speaks to us by his example of faith.

HEBREWS 11:4

*Dear Jesus, help me see the heart of faith through
this difficult and disturbing story so that I
might be encouraged rather than confused.*

The LORD doesn't see things the way you see
them. People judge by outward appearance,
but the LORD looks at the heart.

1 SAMUEL 16:7

In the first recorded murder in the Bible, Cain killed
his brother Abel out of jealousy because Abel offered a
better sacrifice to God than Cain did (Genesis 4). There
are a lot of questions about why Abel's offering was accepted and Cain's wasn't, but the verse in Hebrews sheds
light on this dilemma. It's clear from Hebrews that Abel
gave his offering from a place of faith, and the assump-
tion, therefore, is that Cain did not. This still leaves us

with the questions, What does it mean to bring an offering in faith? And how does that apply to us today?

A faithful offering comes from a place where we recognize God as the giver of every good gift and the source of all good things. It's a recognition that we don't create any good or useful thing on our own, but that the offering only arises from the generous heart of God. A faithful offering then comes from an honest place, where we recognize the kind heart of God toward us even if we aren't feeling particularly cheerful. It comes from a place of gratitude. A faithful offering allows us to acknowledge our dependence on the tenderness of God toward us, causing us to overflow with thankfulness. But still the question remains: since we aren't giving grain or animals in our offerings, what do we give God in faith?

We can give many things to God in faith. We can give our time, honoring God by serving others with a kind heart that reflects Jesus. We can offer our talents and in faith give from our abilities to the furthering of the kingdom of God. We can even give of our finances to demonstrate our reliance upon God for meeting our practical needs.

Perhaps the most powerful thing we can offer to God in faith is our heart. This is a world that is wrecked by sin, and this sin impacts our hearts almost every day. People can wound us with the words they say or the words they withhold that we long to hear. We can be hurt by the choices others make that impact us directly or indirectly. Current events can overwhelm us with fear and anxiety. Every day, we can make a choice to place our hearts into the trustworthy hands of our great Father in heaven. Then our offering will be accepted in faith like Abel, and our lives will be an ongoing testimony to the character of God amid a busted world.

Answer the following questions as honestly as you can. What are the stressors that pull your heart away from trusting in God? Who are the people you are holding anger toward that you need to forgive? What current events are causing you to be uncomfortable or anxious? Begin the hard work of handing these events and people and stressors over to God. This won't be an easy assignment, and we won't be able to complete this task in a single day. But we can start the journey of giving our hearts to God daily and learning to be like Abel.

_____

_____

_____

_____

_____

_____

_____

_____

_____

_____

*Jesus, I want to give my whole heart to You,
but I confess it's hard. I can't muster up the
strength to do it on my own. Would You meet
me with Your strength and teach me how to
give a faithful offering like Abel? Amen.*

BLESSING

May you begin to step into a faithful giving of your heart
to God every day. May you grow in trust related to the
kindness of God. May you find Him to be ever faithful
and ever kind toward you.

5

IT IS IMPOSSIBLE TO PLEASE GOD WITHOUT FAITH

And it is impossible to please God without
faith. Anyone who wants to come to him
must believe that God exists and that he
rewards those who sincerely seek him.

HEBREWS 11:6

*Dear Jesus, open my heart to understand why
faith is required for me to please God, and
how to have that faith even on dark days.*

If you look for me wholeheartedly, you will find me.

JEREMIAH 29:13

Sometimes the Bible seems unreasonable. If faith
isn't part of what I'm feeling today, does this mean
I am incapable of pleasing God? If we are supposed to
have faith even when we aren't feeling it on a given day, it
seems as if God is being arbitrary and harsh, instead of the
caring, loving God we are used to experiencing. And yet,
there must be something to this idea that we need faith to
please God.

The answer comes in looking at the rest of the verse, for
here faith is defined in a very specific way. Rather than
faith being described as the evidence of things hoped for,
here we see faith defined as believing that God exists and

that He rewards those who seek Him. Stated differently, we must believe that God is real and that He is good.

This feels a lot less unreachable than at first glance, but there are still days where we question His character. On the days when the bottom falls out of our life—lost jobs, a child's death, a major depressive episode—we don't know what to think. We can't see up from down or left from right. How exactly are we supposed to know *what* we believe about God in the moment?

Emotions are powerful movers and shakers in our lives, aren't they? When we are overcome by emotions, it's hard to see past them to what we really believe. How can we, for example, really trust in a good God on the day that our wife gets a cancer diagnosis? If God is good, why didn't He stop cancer from taking root in the first place? Or why didn't He vaporize it before the scan confirmed anything? Or why doesn't He jump into the fray and heal her now? Where exactly is this good God during a disaster?

The emotions we are feeling in these dark seasons can draw us away from God in frustration, or they can draw us closer to Him in desperation. But we must do the work of preparing our hearts ahead of time to be ready for a difficulty to arise, because we can be certain it will come. This preparation fundamentally involves knowing ourselves and our tendencies.

When it comes to knowing ourselves, we can be fairly certain that we will respond with the same emotions to many different difficult circumstances. The trick becomes learning our instincts. If we generally respond to bad circumstances with fear, then we can prepare for the fear to show up when difficulties arise. The same can be done for anger, anxiety, depression, and any other response.

We just need to know where our emotions will show up and be prepared for them.

Think back to the last unfortunate event that took place in your life, when you might have been tempted to run from God. Being as specific as possible, what were your emotions telling you at that moment? What do you know to be true about God that can counteract these emotionally charged sentiments?

_____

_____

_____

_____

_____

_____

_____

_____

_____

_____

_____

_____

_____

_____

_____

_____

_____

_____

_____

_____

_____

_____

_____

_____

_____

_____

Jesus, give me the heart to see Your
movement in my life so that when difficult
times come and my emotions want me
to run away from You, I can choose
instead to run toward You. Amen.

BLESSING

May your eyes be opened to see the work of God in your life. May your heart be tender toward Him, causing you to draw near in your difficulties. May your spirit be protected from emotional strain and harm.

6

GOD REWARDS
THOSE WHO SEEK HIM

And it is impossible to please God without
faith. Anyone who wants to come to him
must believe that God exists and that he
rewards those who sincerely seek him.

HEBREWS 11:6

*Dear Jesus, give me eyes to see what it means to be
rewarded by You, and what it doesn't mean as well.*

So let's not get tired of doing what is good.
At just the right time we will reap a harvest
of blessing if we don't give up.

GALATIANS 6:9

It's tricky to gauge how God rewards people. In the Old
Testament, the patriarchs were by and large wealthy, but
this doesn't translate into the New Testament. As a matter
of fact, Jesus asked a young man to sell his possessions to
become a disciple, and in another place, Jesus states that
it is very difficult for the rich to enter heaven. Even James
calls out the hypocrisy of giving special attention to the
rich church members compared to the poor. What are we
to do with all this information, and what does it mean to
be blessed by God?

Galatians 6 gives us a hint by telling us we will reap a

harvest of blessing if we don't give up. Two components are highlighted in this verse related to being blessed by God. The first is that blessing doesn't come right away. We are told not to give up, which implies that there is a waiting time between when we sow what is good and when we reap the harvest of blessing. We need to keep on being good-hearted, kind, generous people, moving in accordance with God's calling in our lives. Eventually, we will begin to see the fruit of that hard work.

The second thing we see from this verse is that God gives the fruit of the harvest from what we have spent time planting. We have to ask ourselves this powerful question: What can we anticipate being the fruit of planting good works? The answers can be limitless but at least include three possibilities. One fruit of good works might be a good reputation. Just as the patriarchs earned a good reputation by honoring God with their lives, we may be seen as positive lights in our spheres of influence. This could include your neighborhood, your children's school, your workplace, or even your church. Over time, people may know that you are trustworthy and kind.

The second fruit of good works is kindness returned. The Proverbs are chock-full of statements about the wise receiving the goodness of their wisdom back into their lives. In the same way, your good works could be reciprocated in a variety of ways. It might be anything, a plate of cookies from the neighbor or a raise at work.

The third fruit of good works is less obvious but just as important. You will have the privilege of participating in the works of God alongside of God (2 Corinthians 5:17–20). The love of God will rest upon your spirit in a unique way as you develop a kinship with Him by pursuing good deeds and kindness in your everyday life. You will begin to walk in an intimacy that is new and exciting because you are reflecting His heart in your life (1 John 4:12–13).

We are quick in Christianity to label good works as a bad thing because of their link to legalism, but this just isn't accurate. Good works are a wonderful way to show our devotion to our amazing Savior, and it's only when we use them as spiritual collateral or proof of our own goodness that they pose any problem at all.

It's time to get serious about goodness now. What are some practical things you can do today or tomorrow that would sow good works? How can you make a positive impact in your community and your workplace and anywhere else you have influence? Write down at least five ideas, then commit to doing at least two of them in the next month.

_____

_____

_____

_____

_____

_____

_____

_____

_____

_____

_____

_____

_____

_____

_____

_____

_____

_____

_____

_____

_____

*Jesus, give me the eyes to see where I
can leave a trail of goodness behind
me. Give me the vision to change my
environment in positive ways. Amen.*

BLESSING

May you stop underestimating the difference you can
make in this world. May you begin to see the fruit of
sowing goodness daily. May you have an unquenchable
desire to see the kingdom of God expand in every part
of your life.

7

NOAH BELIEVED GOD FOR THE FIRST RAIN EVER

It was by faith that Noah built a large boat to save his
family from the flood. He obeyed God, who warned
him about things that had never happened before. By
his faith Noah condemned the rest of the world, and
he received the righteousness that comes by faith.

HEBREWS 11:7

*Dear Jesus, give me a heart like Noah, who
believed You when You said something that
Noah had no frame of reference for. Give me
faith that isn't based on my understanding of
things but is based on who I know You to be.*

So Noah did everything exactly as
God had commanded him.

GENESIS 6:22

Has God ever asked you to do something truly
crazy? If not, reread the full story of Noah for some
perspective (Genesis 7:1–9:17). God told Noah He was
going to flood the earth with rain from heaven, but it had
never rained before. It's hard for us to imagine a world
without rain, but this is what we have in the pre-flood
world. If you read the Genesis story carefully, you will
see that water came up from the ground and no rain was

necessary. Again, this sounds like science fiction to us, but a serious reading of the Bible points us to this conclusion.

Noah was told that the entire world was going to be flooded with water from above and water from below, but he had never seen rain before, much less a flood of any type. Then we must add to the mix that God said all sorts of animals were going to be sent to Noah to fit into the ark he was given instructions to build. This whole scenario almost reads as ridiculous, but Noah didn't take it that way at all. Instead, he responded in obedience to all the Lord had commanded him to do.

Noah stands as a testimony to us today, all these years later. God isn't going to ask any of us to build an ark when it's never rained before, but He will call us to step out in faith into situations that feel scary to us. Whether it's sharing our faith story with a coworker or choosing to be more generous with our finances, God is always calling us into a deeper journey of faith. We can look to Noah as an example of how to respond when it seems like God is calling us to something a little bit crazy. Like Noah, we can obey everything God has said to us, and like Noah, we will receive the righteousness that comes from faith.

Beyond righteousness, we can gain so much more as well. Noah learned that God always keeps His promises, no matter how radical. The same is true for us—the more we trust God in seemingly crazy circumstances, the more we will see His trustworthiness, and the more we can continue to trust Him moving forward. Building a personal history of how God has been faithful to us is a powerful conduit for our own faithfulness to Him.

When we read Noah's story, one thing that stands out is that he never asked to build an ark. Instead, he just honored God with his life, and he caught God's eye as a result. We can do the same.

Think back on your history with God. What seemingly crazy thing or things has He asked you to do? What was the result of those crazy things, and how did God show Himself to be faithful? What did you learn about God as a result of being faithful in following Him? Or conversely, what opportunities might you have missed by stepping away from radical obedience? Write down all these experiences and the lessons you've learned from being obedient (or not) to what God has called you into.

_____

_____

_____

_____

_____

_____

_____

_____

_____

_____

_____

_____

_____

_____

_____

_____

_____

_____

_____

_____

_____

_____

Jesus, I don't want to miss any more opportunities to be obedient to what You want me to do. Would You trust me with something clear and obvious to me, so that I can know the exhilaration of seeing You do something radical and unexpected? Amen.

BLESSING

May you catch the attention of God's heart with your love for Him. May you learn how to risk for Jesus, even if you do it afraid. May you step into the wild and crazy life of listening to God and responding with a heart of obedience.

8

ABRAM DIDN'T KNOW WHERE HE WAS GOING

It was by faith that Abraham obeyed when God
called him to leave home and go to another land
that God would give him as his inheritance. He
went without knowing where he was going.

HEBREWS 11:8

*Dear Jesus, remove from my heart the need
to always know the end from the beginning
when You call me to something new.*

The LORD had said to Abram, "Leave your native
country, your relatives, and your father's family,
and go to the land that I will show you."

GENESIS 12:1

Leave behind everything familiar. Imagine for a moment that God tells you in no uncertain terms to move away from your home, your city, your state, and your extended family. What would likely be the first question you had of God? I'm guessing it would be, Where are we going, God? Two things stick out about this story: God didn't tell Abram where he was going, and Abram never asked (you can read about the start of Abram's journey in Genesis 12).

He left his community and his sense of comfort and safety for a place God was going to show him.

Another thing that is worth noting here is that Abram was seventy-five years old when God called him into an adventure. This story feels like something a twenty-something might pursue, but that's not the story we are given. Abram was settled into the beginning of his twilight years. I'm sure he was comfortable living in Haran, where he'd been most of his life. And yet he dropped everything in response to the call of God to go somewhere else, somewhere uncertain.

Maybe the promises God gave to Abram after asking him to leave Haran convinced Abram to leave his comfortable retirement home and venture into the great unknown. After all, God did tell Abram that he would be a great nation, that he would be a blessing to others, and that all families on Earth would be blessed through him. Those are high goals for anyone's life, and it could have been enough to convince him to leave everything.

We don't know how God spoke to Abram. Perhaps it was through a dream or a vision. Maybe God spoke to Abram through a burning bush as He did later with Moses. Even an angel could have come and spoken to him. This is a mystery that isn't answered in the Bible. But one thing we do know is that however God spoke to Abram, it was convincing enough for him to drop the comforts of home and follow God's call on his life.

Regardless of the reasons, whether it was the method God spoke to him or the promises given, Abram was convinced. He left familiarity for an unknown future. Sometimes God calls us to the same thing—He calls us out of our normal and into a radical adventure. These are both exciting and terrifying times. It's exciting because we don't know what the future holds, and it's terrifying for precisely the same reason. As humans we tend to try to focus on safety and security. Walking into a season of unknowns feels uncomfortable. And yet, this might be the very reason God pushes us into these new seasons. If we aren't comfortable, then it's that much more difficult to lean into our own expertise, and that much more likely that we will instead lean into God and in His providence for our security.

Ask God this terrifying question: What adventure would you have me engage in? Be ready to hear something small or something radical because either is a distinct possibility. God could call you to move to Portland to plant a house church or maybe He will just tell you it's time to take your new coworker out to lunch to learn a little more about her. Knowing that anything is on the table can be intimidating, but it's still vital to come to God with an open and willing heart. As you stay in a position of openness to God, write down the direction to which you feel God is inviting you, and decide to do what He's put on your heart.

_____

_____

_____

_____

_____

_____

_____

_____

_____

_____

_____

*Jesus, give me a heart of courage like
Abram—free me to follow You no matter
what the cost is. Whether that means
doing something simple or out of the
ordinary, I want to be obedient to fulfilling
whatever You ask of me. Teach me
obedience and faithfulness to You. Amen.*

BLESSING

May you develop a greater sense of what God is calling
you to do, regardless of what season of life you're in
right now. May you wholeheartedly follow God, whatever the cost. May you choose to leave familiarity for
adventure in Christ.

9

ABRAM DWELLED IN TENTS

And even when he [Abram] reached the land God
promised him, he lived there by faith—for he was
like a foreigner, living in tents. And so did Isaac
and Jacob, who inherited the same promise.

HEBREWS 11:9

*Dear Jesus, like Abram I am walking in the promised
land of my inheritance but not receiving it in full.
Teach me to wait patiently for the full inheritance.*

When they arrived in Canaan, Abram traveled
through the land as far as Shechem. There he
set up camp beside the oak of Moreh.

GENESIS 12:5−6

Did God make a mistake? Abram left what was familiar to follow the call of God for his life. After some time, he arrived in the land God promised him, and then . . . nothing happened. He didn't receive his inheritance in any way. He didn't have the land of Canaan handed to him on a silver platter. He wasn't even given the option of fighting for his inheritance. Literally nothing happened. If you read more in the Genesis story, you will see that Abram continued to move from place to place within Canaan. Eventually, he found a place to settle for a bit longer, but it was still in tents.

It must have been a difficult transition for Abram and

Sarai. Surely, they had a more permanent home in Haran, especially since Abram's father, Terah, had also lived in Haran. Adjusting to a mobile lifestyle must have felt like a downgrade in terms of lifestyle and comfort for them, with multiple inconveniences. Moving from place to place was no simple matter, made even more difficult by a large household with servants and flocks to consider. Yet Abram and Sarai continued to do just that, seeking the will and heart of God for him and his family.

I wonder how it felt for Abram to be a foreigner in the land that he knew was his inheritance? It must have been frustrating some of the time. He would look at the Canaanites living in their cities with their houses and other proof of permanent dwellings. The Canaanites could walk to their fields and pick fruit for dinner, then walk back to their house. Abram could do none of these things because he hadn't received his inheritance; it was just a promise.

This can feel very familiar. God has promised the hope of heaven, but in the meantime, we might look like fools for following an invisible God. God has said we will have an abundant life, but sometimes we walk in want instead. God has told us in His Bible that generosity is rewarded for the faithful, but, on occasion, we might think it would be easier if we stopped tithing and neglected giving to ministries to free us to go on more expensive vacations or any vacation at all, to have more reliable transportation, or to pay for better clothes for our kids.

Like Abram, many of us are pitching tents in the land of our inheritance and living as foreigners, not reaping the benefits of the promises of God. Sometimes, this is a function of that busted world we talked about in the introduction, and we have no choice but to wait until the world is set right. There are also times when we can begin the hard work of preparing a foundation and laying the groundwork for freedom in our lives today.

What promise or promises from God do you feel are left unfulfilled for you? Where do you feel as if God has let you down? In what area of life do you feel like you are dwelling in a tent when you feel you should be able to live in a city? It's okay to be honest about this—God can handle our frustration with Him, and even welcomes it. The first step toward understanding where freedom is available to us is to identify where we feel trapped.

_____

_____

_____

_____

_____

_____

_____

_____

_____

_____

_____

_____

_____

_____

_____

_____

_____

_____

_____

_____

Jesus, give me the courage to ask You for the freedom I desperately long for. Whether I live in a so-called tent or a palace on this side of eternity, show me the next steps to having a more fulfilled life as I walk through my own Canaan. Amen.

BLESSING

May you see the details of your own inheritance in your own Canaan. May you begin to yearn for freedom instead of accepting tents in your life. May you see that freedom in your life soon.

10

ABRAHAM LOOKED FORWARD TO GOD'S CITY

Abraham was confidently looking forward to a city with
eternal foundations, a city designed and built by God.

HEBREWS 11:10

*Dear Jesus, I want to have a sense of Your grand
and beautiful future for me in order to push through
dark times when they come and not lose heart.*

And I saw the holy city, the new Jerusalem,
coming down from God out of heaven like a
bride beautifully dressed for her husband.

REVELATION 21:2

Abraham's life was no picnic. We don't get the inside
scoop on a lot of the daily details of his life, but I'm
certain there were dark days. Not just in the big moments
told in Scripture, for instance when Lot was captured by
enemy forces, but darkness in the everyday moments of
life too. Those days when the promises of land and a son
seemed far away and unreachable. He must have felt overwhelmed on some days when he was traveling from one
end of Canaan to another, seeking the will of God for his
life and his family.

Yet we read in Hebrews 11:10 that he confidently
looked toward the future, and this future was more than

the initial promises given to him by God. He was able to see that God was building a grand future for him that had nothing to do with the specific promises of a son and land. He knew that God was at work creating an amazing inheritance for him, even when it looked like nothing was happening. To be sure, Abraham had his missteps and sins. How could we forget about his decision to sleep with Hagar to get a son when Sarah was barren? How could we overlook his decision to call Sarah his sister instead of his wife to protect his own hide? Yet the Bible tells us that he confidently looked forward to the city God was building.

We can have that same hope when the days trend badly for us. When all hope seems to be running away from us and the good times are nothing but a distant memory, we can be confident that God is in the process right now of building that city for us. There will be a day when wrongs are made right, when injustices are set aside, when recompense is given, when all is forgiven, when tears will be dried, and when pain will disappear. There will be a day when God triumphantly brings us to the new heavenly Jerusalem, where there is no need for the sun because the glory of God is all the light we need.

When perseverance runs thin and when hope seems gone, we can look forward to this ultimate destination of our souls and bodies and take heart.

Write out the words of Revelation 21:4–5. It might feel weird to just copy the words of the Bible, but there is a power that comes in writing out verses. It solidifies in our brains the things we are reading. This exercise will help you to recognize and reflect on the amazing future God has planned for you. He is going to live in your midst. He is going to banish pain and death and sorrow. This is the plan in place for your future, and it's spectacular.

_____

_____

_____

_____

_____

_____

_____

_____

_____

_____

_____

*Jesus, give me a vision for the grand future
You have for me in the new heavens and the
new earth, and allow this vision to inspire me
to keep going when things are tough. Amen.*

BLESSING

May you find hope in the future inheritance God has for you in the new heavens and the new earth. May you be encouraged by considering this future in your dark moments. May you, like Abraham, confidently wait to see the designs of God unfold in your life.

11

SARAH BECAME A MOTHER IN HER OLD AGE

It was by faith that even Sarah was able to have a
child, though she was barren and was too old.

HEBREWS 11:11

*Dear Jesus, remind me that I am never too old
to experience the blessings and favor of God
in my life—even if it doesn't make any natural
sense and seems worth laughing about.*

So [Sarah] laughed silently to herself and
said, "How could a worn-out woman like
me enjoy such pleasure, especially when my
master—my husband—is also so old?"

GENESIS 18:12

Sarah was no superhero. She was a normal person,
just like all of us. She defined herself in light of her
physical characteristics: her age, her body image, and her
ability to have children. She called herself a "worn-out
woman," and the insinuation is clear (Genesis 18:12).
At ninety years of age, Sarah thought her longings and
dreams were past their expiration date. She must have
thought that there was no way that she could become a
mother. Her time had passed long ago, and on the surface,
she seemed to be content with that.

But was she really? She must have known that her husband had been promised a son. She was surely aware of the shame that barren women carried in her culture, and she must have secretly hoped for a miracle. Or maybe she really had given up on the idea of being a mother. The Bible is silent on what Sarah thought when the angels visited Abraham in Genesis 18, except that she laughed. But that laugh could have been born out of the bitterness of a childless life, or it could have been the result of simply doing the math on her age, near 90 years old, and Abraham's age, near 100, or maybe it was a laugh that did hope against hope that these angels did know what they were talking about. We see that God confronted her for her laughter, so that gives us some insight that it was born out of a lack of faith, but we will never know for sure on this side of heaven.

What we do know is that the angels promised her a son within a year, and that's exactly what happened. In that situation, God wasn't bound by physiological barriers to motherhood. He had a promise to fulfill, and He was all about keeping His promise to Abraham and Sarah. He even sent angels to visit them to set a timeline for His miracle to take place. God was serious about keeping His promise, and He wanted to make sure they knew that—even if it meant His angels got laughed at in the process.

The Bible tells us that Jesus is the same yesterday, today, and forever (see Hebrews 13:8). God is still in the business of keeping His promises. He still moves in ways that defy explanation. He is still unbound by normal circumstances that might stump a scientist. He is still working miracles today to fulfill His promises.

What promises are you waiting for God to fulfill in

your life? Maybe you feel like life has passed you by. Like Sarah, maybe you think you're nothing but a worn-out person waiting out the rest of your days. Perhaps you question whether someone as good as God would even want anything to do with someone like you, with all your mistakes and pains and hang-ups. God's promise to you, to all of us really, is that He is looking to give us good things to enjoy. Like Sarah, we might feel like we aren't worthy, but the good news is that receiving His gifts isn't about being worthy. It's about God being faithful to His promises.

Answer these questions as honestly as you can, without holding anything back. Where do you feel like God has left you behind? What promises would you be ready to laugh about if He were to reengage you in them? It's been mentioned before, but it is worth repeating: God can handle our brutal honesty.

_____

_____

_____

_____

_____

_____

_____

_____

_____

_____

_____

_____

_____

_____

Now that you've been raw and real in articulating your responses, it's time for the hard work of bringing this before God in prayer. Perhaps it will come with some anguish and confusion, but ask God to help you understand why His promises haven't been fulfilled in your life.

> *Jesus, I don't want to be left behind,*
> *but I feel like that's exactly what is*
> *happening in my life. Would You remind*
> *me that You are always faithful and will*
> *fulfill Your promises to me? Amen.*

BLESSING

May you have the courage to be honest with God about feeling left behind. May you feel free to question and to invite candid conversation with God about whether He is still faithfully working in your life. May you experience the renewed joy that comes with a long-forgotten promise being fulfilled.

12

ABRAHAM BECAME FATHER TO US ALL

And so a whole nation came from this one man who was as good as dead—a nation with so many people that, like the stars in the sky and the sand on the seashore, there is no way to count them.

HEBREWS 11:12

Dear Jesus, teach us to have faith like Abraham, a faith that grows stronger as the days carry on.

Even when there was no reason for hope, Abraham kept hoping—believing that he would become the father of many nations. For God had said to him, "That's how many descendants you will have!"

ROMANS 4:18

Abraham laughed at God. He chuckled at the promise given to him by God for a son because he was bound by his earthly understanding of what was possible and what was impossible (Genesis 17:15–22). He knew that he was an old man, that Sarah was an old woman, and that it just didn't make sense for them to have a child. Abraham almost immediately started suggesting alternatives. First, he suggested that his chief servant could be his heir and receive the inheritance promised by God. Then, he tried sleeping with another woman to achieve the purposes of

God. But eventually, Abraham came to see that God was fully able to accomplish what He had promised, regardless of how impossible or even absurd it seemed. And it was then that God fulfilled His promise to Abraham.

Abraham needed to grow in his faith toward God, to give God a chance to fulfill His promises. In the beginning, Abraham wasn't leaving space for God to work because Abraham was convinced he could figure it all out on his own. While God can obviously move in any environment, this left God on the outside looking in on Abraham's life. He tried to help God fulfill His promise, but God didn't need or even want that help. Instead, Abraham just showed his lack of faith. In time, Abraham learned to leave the miracle-working to God, and he received his promised son.

We can take the same approach as Abraham if we aren't careful. We can go about the business of trying to make the perfect environment for God to work, instead of standing back and letting God be God. We can use logic and reason to crowd God out, leaving Him on the outskirts of our lives. We can follow the early example of Abraham and try to work things out in our own power. Or we can trust that God will work in His own time to accomplish His purposes. Only once we stop such activities and give God permission to move can He work more fully in our lives. Failing to do this can extend periods of unfruitfulness and can actually keep God from working powerfully in our midst.

It's confession time. This is going to be rough, but it will be worth it in the end. As you think back over the last three months, where have you tried to "play God"? Where have you tried to fill in the blanks and to be the miracle worker in your life? Write down what you realize as you ponder these deep questions. Confess to God that you're sorry that you've tried to take His place in your life, and commit to letting God be the decision-maker moving forward.

_____

_____

_____

_____

_____

_____

_____

_____

_____

_____

_____

_____

_____

_____

_____

_____

_____

_____

_____

_____

_____

_____

_____

_____

_____

_____

*Jesus, I want to grow in my faith as
Abraham did throughout his life. Forgive
me for trying to play God in my life,
and teach me to look for opportunities
to let You lead instead. Amen.*

BLESSING

May you see God as the one who can work every possible miracle to accomplish His purpose in your life. May you grow in your faith day by day as Abraham did. May you have the courage to step back and patiently wait on God's timing for His promises to you.

13

OUR ANCESTORS DID NOT RECEIVE THEIR PROMISES

All these people died still believing what
God had promised them. They did not
receive what was promised, but they saw it
all from a distance and welcomed it.

HEBREWS 11:13

*Dear Jesus, allow my faith to rest on what I know
You have promised to be true instead of what I see
with my eyes concerning my present circumstances.*

For we live by believing and not by seeing.

2 CORINTHIANS 5:7

What a good resting place Hebrews 11:13 is to reflect on the faith heroes we have discussed already and consider their similarities. Abel gave an offering out of a heart of faith, not necessarily understanding the significance of his offering. It's important to note that nowhere in the Bible do we see instructions given to Abel or Cain about how or what to offer to God, so there may have been some sense of mystery around God's response to the offerings. Whether God gave instructions unrecorded by Scripture or there were no instructions at all, Abel seemed to believe God would reward him for his offering. Yet this faithful offering provoked Cain's jealousy of his right standing with God, ultimately leading to Abel's murder at the hands of his brother.

Noah had a heart for long obedience toward God and, as a result, acted on God's promises to him. He was given specific instructions by God on how to build the ark, and this was no small undertaking. Building an ark that is over four hundred feet long took some time, and we have no record that Noah ever wavered. He trusted God by looking to the promises spoken over him instead of look- ing to the things he could see. Noah is the exception to our Hebrews verse because he did receive the protection promised by God, but it still took time for him to see the fruit of his obedience.

Together, Sarah and Abraham undertook a spectacu- lar adventure with God, based solely on His promises. They left what was familiar to them, entrusting that God would provide a land as an inheritance to them. They trusted God to provide a son, despite their advanced age. They definitely made mistakes along the way, but never- theless continued with steadfast hearts to follow God and believe in His promises. Nearly twenty years after obeying the initial call to leave their home, part of their promise was fulfilled in the birth of Isaac. As with Noah, it took long obedience toward God to see that promise. And the promise of the land as an inheritance wouldn't be fulfilled for hundreds of years, after the enslavement of his descendants for generations.

We must remember this concept of long obedience when times feel dark for us, when the promises of God seem far away, or when we wonder where God is in our lives. There are seasons where we are preparing a sac- rifice for Him and the reward might be the death of a dream, but on the other side of that death awaits intimacy with God. There are times when we are obeying blindly in ways that don't make sense to us, but the fruit of that obedience will be radical deliverance and opportunities to go on an adventure with Him. Sometimes God calls us to leave what is comfortable with little to depend on except His promises. While it can be intimidating to follow God wholeheartedly, the life change that comes as a result is undeniable.

Reflect on where God is calling you to long obedience and the challenges you've faced along the way. Where has God seemed silent, and how have you responded to this silence? When have the promises of God felt lifeless and distant? Ask the Lord to rekindle hope and passion for you in these promises and in His goodness.

_____

_____

_____

_____

_____

_____

_____

_____

_____

_____

*Jesus, sometimes long obedience is hard.
I'm exerting all my energy to just put
one foot in front of the other, and I still
can't seem to find You. Help me to see
how You've been by my side, even when
You've felt distant from me. Amen.*

BLESSING

May you, like Abel, offer a better sacrifice. May you, like
Noah, push forward into a new thing based on the promised deliverance of God. May you, like Abraham, find new
adventures in obedience.

14

WE ARE MEMBERS OF GOD'S FAMILY

They agreed that they were foreigners and nomads here
on earth. Obviously people who say such things are
looking forward to a country they can call their own.

HEBREWS 11:13–14

*Dear Jesus, remind us of what it means to be
part of the family of God in a real and tangible
way, involved in a safe space that allows us to
thrive and be truly known in vulnerability.*

So now you Gentiles are no longer strangers and
foreigners. You are citizens along with all of God's
holy people. You are members of God's family.

EPHESIANS 2:19

Ever feel alone on this planet? It's far too easy to feel
like a nomad on planet Earth, to not know where we
belong or where to turn for comfort and encouragement
when life is challenging. Like the heroes of Hebrews 11,
we see ourselves as foreigners everywhere we go, with
no place to call home: We have many acquaintances but
rarely feel truly known, our workplaces are rife with com-
petition rather than camaraderie, and our churches can
be, at times, more concerned with attendance than pas-
toral care. We can feel alone, adrift in a sea of loneliness

to fend for ourselves as part of the so-called dream of independence. What if this wasn't the way God called us to live? What if there was a different way?

In this book, we have been drawing from the examples of the very real people found in Hebrews 11 to find encouragement and strength, but we have to part ways with them here. The clear teaching of the New Testament is that we are not alone, but we are members of God's family. We have a place to call our home—the church. We have citizenship in God's kingdom, but what does this mean, and how does it look in our daily lives?

Being citizens in God's kingdom involves a lot of things, but at the very least it affirms we have a free pass to the throne of grace in times of need (Hebrews 4:16). We have access to the King of the universe and can seek His help when we are overwhelmed. This is powerful, something we too often overlook or view as a last resort. How often have you tried everything else, so you guess the only thing left to try is prayer? Being a citizen of heaven means that we can start with the Creator of all things when we're struggling with something (Philippians 4:6–7). We can bring our trials to Him and seek His help, and He promises to listen and act on our behalf. What a powerful thought!

Being citizens in God's kingdom also means that we are not alone in this world (John 14:18). We share citizenship with everyone else who claims Christ as the Lord of their life (Philippians 3:20). We can reach out to our fellow believers and ask for help and support. Sometimes that support will look like a meal for our family when we are in the hospital, and other times it might look like a prayer when we are depressed. It could even be a hug on a hard day. Our fellow citizens are here to support us in our hard moments, because we are not foreigners or nomads like our ancestors (Galatians 6:2). We belong to God and to His kingdom.

There are two application points for today. First, I want you to write down the struggles you've been afraid to share with God. Let me remind you again that God is not intimidated or frustrated by our struggles. On the contrary, He loves when we trust Him with our hard times. After you've written them down, bring them before God. This prayer can be as simple as this: "God, here are my struggles. Please help me."

The second application point is to identify one person you are going to trust with one of your struggles, or who you are going to trust the next time you hit a tough time. If you live like a nomad, commit to yourself and to God that you will invest in friendships with other citizens in God's kingdom.

_____

_____

_____

_____

_____

_____

_____

_____

_____

_____

_____

*Jesus, I want to trust You and others more—
help me to stop living as a foreigner and
to plant roots in Your kingdom. Amen.*

BLESSING

May you find the courage to step into the throne room
of God with your struggles, no matter how small or
how overwhelming they might feel to you. May you find
people to trust in when life gets difficult. May you begin
to experience the joy of being a citizen of God's kingdom.

15

ABRAHAM NEVER TURNED BACK

If they had longed for the country they came
from, they could have gone back. But they were
looking for a better place, a heavenly homeland.
That is why God is not ashamed to be called their
God, for he has prepared a city for them.

HEBREWS 11:15–16

*Dear Jesus, teach me to lean forward in
anticipation of Your coming rather than
shrinking back in hesitation and fear.*

And now, dear children, remain in fellowship with
Christ so that when he returns, you will be full of
courage and not shrink back from him in shame.

1 JOHN 2:28

The life of Abraham is remarkable because we
never read of him turning back from the promise of
God to inherit a land and have a son. Nowhere in the
pages of Genesis do we read of a conversation between
Abraham and Sarah where they considered returning
to Haran because he was tired of wandering the land
of Canaan. Unlike the Israelites under the leadership
of Moses, Abraham never seemed to complain about
how easy life was back in Haran. He never said that he

missed having a house to call his own, a comfortable chair to recline in at the end of the day, and a certainty about where tomorrow would take him.

Instead, we see that Abraham leaned into the uncertainty that was part of his life with God. We have to read a little into his story to see this, but each time Abraham built an altar, there's a likelihood he was seeking direction from God on where to go next. Imagine not knowing where tomorrow would take you or where you would lay your head at the end of the day. Imagine not having a house to return to, but instead only a tent—the most temporary of dwellings. It is because of this determination to stay faithful to God that the prophet Isaiah called Abraham the "friend" of God (Isaiah 41:8).

We have this same opportunity to be a friend of God if we, like Abraham, will lean into our future. There is a lot that is undetermined in every person's life. Who knows when a job will end, or a loved one will have an unexpected illness beset them, or a marriage will fall apart seemingly out of nowhere? In all these circumstances and more, we have a choice: We can lean forward into the promises of God, or we can shrink back in confusion and shame. Leaning forward is a tough choice to activate, but its root is very simple. The root of leaning forward is asking this one question: God, what are you doing in this dark season? Or, what do you want me to know right now in the midst of my struggles? God is often faithful to answer these questions, but our role is to continue to pray and to seek Him, whether He answers or not.

Be transparent, and write down the questions you have for God about the dark seasons of your life. Ask the tough questions about why the pain was so intense and lasting. Confess your desire to shrink back from God in frustration, pain, or aggravation in those moments when God has felt silent or absent.

_____

_____

_____

_____

_____

_____

_____

_____

_____

_____

_____

*Jesus, there are times I have shrunk back
from You and desired to return to my own
Haran instead of following You into the
next adventure that You have for me. Teach
me to trust You more, that I might be called
a friend of God like Abraham. Amen.*

BLESSING

May you find the strength to ask God the hard questions
about why He sometimes seems far away. May you have
the patience to wait for His answers. May you keep moving
forward toward your Canaan as you wait.

16

ABRAHAM PASSED GOD'S TEST

It was by faith that Abraham offered Isaac as a sacrifice when God was testing him. Abraham, who had received God's promises, was ready to sacrifice his only son, Isaac, even though God had told him, "Isaac is the son through whom your descendants will be counted." Abraham reasoned that if Isaac died, God was able to bring him back to life again. And in a sense, Abraham did receive his son back from the dead.

HEBREWS 11:17–19

Dear Jesus, I know a difficult test is either coming or has already passed. Give me the eyes to see when the testing is coming, and the faith to pass the test as Abraham did.

Abraham named the place Yahweh-Yireh (which means "the LORD will provide"). To this day, people still use that name as a proverb: "On the mountain of the LORD it will be provided."

GENESIS 22:14

God sometimes asks for the nearly impossible. We can't underestimate the sorrow that could have accompanied Abraham on his journey to the mountain to sacrifice his son to God (see Genesis 22:1–19 for the full story). This was Isaac, whom he had waited over twenty years for. This was the promised son from God, through whom Abraham would become the father of many nations. Isaac was also his only remaining son, as Ishmael had already been sent off with his mother.

The story in Genesis is silent on what was in Abraham's head. What he experienced as he traveled with his son and his servants to Mount Moriah is unimaginable. He did have faith that God was going to do something miraculous because he told his servants that he and Isaac would return. But that expectation might have been tinged with confusion and perhaps doubt as well. Abraham could have been wondering what God was up to when Isaac questioned him about where the sacrifice was going to come from. Maybe Abraham turned away from Isaac to hide his tears as he said that God would provide the burnt offering. Abraham could have even been weeping as he laid Isaac upon the altar and raised his knife, wondering what God was doing. Hebrews 11:19 tells us that Abraham believed God could raise Isaac, which lowers the stakes somewhat, but Abraham and Isaac would still be stuck with the memory of him plunging the knife into his son's chest—not the stuff of bedtime stories.

It was at this last moment that God showed up and told Abraham to stop, pointing him instead to a ram. What would have happened if Abraham had stopped listening for the voice of God in that moment? He would have killed his son Isaac for no reason. Here is the lesson for us. We must never stop listening for the heartbeat of God, no matter how dire our external circumstances appear—even if it seems our dreams have been sacrificed. We can never be sure when God will show up with a proverbial ram to rescue us from pain or to restore us.

We might look at the story of Abraham and Isaac with

scorn. I know I have. How dare God test Abraham's faith in such a ridiculous way? What could God possibly need to see at this moment that He couldn't intuit from reading Abraham's heart since He is all-knowing? This same pain can accompany our own stories of sacrifice as we wonder where God was and why He allowed such sorrow.

Write down the most painful moments you've experienced in your life. It could be the betrayal of a close friend, the death of your spouse, or a failed ministry opportunity. Whatever it is, write it down in as much detail as you can muster. Then ask God why He allowed it to happen. You might not get an answer, but then again you might, and it could be a salve for the deep wounds you've carried around for too long. Asking God the tough questions is how we learn the answers and draw close to God.

_____

_____

_____

_____

_____

_____

_____

_____

_____

_____

_____

*Jesus, I've been in the land of Moriah, and
I've wondered where You were as I raised
the proverbial knife to sacrifice important
things, even promised things. Give me eyes
to see what You were trying to accomplish
through this pain. I'm tired of hurting. Amen.*

BLESSING

May you learn to trust God as you climb Mount Moriah.
May you learn with Abraham the power of Yahweh-Yireh. May you hear the heartbeat of God for you again.

17

GOD COULD HAVE BROUGHT ISAAC BACK TO LIFE

Abraham reasoned that if Isaac died, God was able
to bring him back to life again. And in a sense,
Abraham did receive his son back from the dead.

HEBREWS 11:19

*Dear Jesus, I want to see my dreams
brought back to life as Abraham saw Isaac
brought back from the brink of death.*

Now all glory to God, who is able, through his
mighty power at work within us, to accomplish
infinitely more than we might ask or think.

EPHESIANS 3:20

Abraham had never faced a moment like this before. As we talked about in the last devotion, Abraham was told by God to sacrifice his son, the epitome of
the promises of God, to kill his dream quite literally (Genesis 22:1–19). We don't gain any insight into the emotions
Abraham was feeling on his way to Mount Moriah, but
his heart might have been breaking as he considered this
course of action. Many questions could have been running
through his mind about the intent and character of God.

For Abraham, the path forward was one of obedience. Despite the conflict he may have felt, Abraham

continued to pursue what God told him to do. When Isaac asked where the sacrifice would come from, Abraham answered as honestly as he could by saying God would provide the sacrifice. Abraham didn't know if God would provide that sacrifice in his son or through some other miracle, but he knew nonetheless that God was going to supply it. Abraham was ready to kill his own son to be obedient to God. How could Abraham be ready for such a choice?

Today's verse in Hebrews 11 shines a light on how Abraham was able and ready to sacrifice Isaac on an altar to God: "Abraham reasoned that if Isaac died, God was able to bring him back to life again" (Hebrews 11:19). In other words, Abraham trusted in the resurrection power of God even in his most trying circumstances. This sounds very much like something Paul said to the Thessalonian church when he told them they shouldn't view death in the same way as those who have no hope (1 Thessalonians 4:13–14), and that's on purpose. Our God is the same throughout all of history. Our God was the same resurrecting God on Mount Moriah that He was three days after the death of Jesus, and He will be the same God at the end of this age when He raises all of us to join Him in the new heavens and new earth.

Just as Abraham believed God was able to resurrect his son Isaac, we too can believe that God is able to resurrect our hopes and dreams when they align with God's will and purposes. We can hold fast to the unending power of our God. This is why Ephesians 3:20 tells us with confidence that God can accomplish more than we can even think to ask. Because of the brokenness of the world, on this side of eternity, dreams may go unfulfilled or may be rechanneled as we discover His greater purposes for us. But our God is a miracle-working God, and that will never change. Even when we experience the despair of busted dreams and a broken life, God can restore them.

Identify your fractured dreams, and give yourself permission to honestly name the areas of your life where you have unfulfilled dreams and longings. We've said this before, but God can handle your outright honesty. He actually encourages it, because it draws you closer to Him. Tell God about your "Isaacs" that have been sacrificed—those dreams, relationships, or things that God hasn't resurrected yet. Ask Him to talk with you about why your life is a bit more broken than you wish it were and to give you insight into what's happening. Listen carefully in your spirit for any guidance that might come in these moments and write down what you hear. Something that is almost always true is this: when we openly ask God for an answer, it is His Spirit we will hear in response to that prayer, not something else. Trust what you hear.

_____

_____

_____

_____

_____

_____

_____

_____

*Jesus, I come to You with my shattered
dreams that cry out for resurrection.
Like the father of the epileptic (Mark
9:24), I believe and ask You to help me
in my unbelief. I want to believe You can
resurrect my life and my dreams when
they align with Your plans and purposes,
but only part of me actually believes.
Bridge the gap for me, O God. Amen.*

BLESSING

May you find answers for your broken dreams in the resurrection power of God. May you hear the heartbeat of
God for you. May you see God meet you in your unbelief and strengthen you with confidence from His throne
room.

18

JACOB BLESSED HIS FAMILY

It was by faith that Isaac promised blessings
for the future to his sons, Jacob and Esau.
It was by faith that Jacob, when he was old
and dying, blessed each of Joseph's sons and
bowed in worship as he leaned on his staff.

HEBREWS 11:20–21

*Dear Jesus, give me a clear vision to see beyond the
end of my own life. I want to be able to forecast
blessings and favor from God to future generations.*

May the God before whom my grandfather
    Abraham
  and my father, Isaac, walked—
the God who has been my shepherd
  all my life, to this very day,
the Angel who has redeemed me from all
    harm—
  may he bless these boys.
May they preserve my name
  and the names of Abraham and Isaac.
And may their descendants multiply greatly
  throughout the earth.

GENESIS 48:15–16

Promising blessings is a lost art. Today, we never
hear of a grandparent spending time blessing his or
her grandchildren, but I think we should. Imagine for a

moment a grandparent speaking words of encouragement in an intentional moment with his or her grandchildren, or maybe a parent choosing to share hopeful things with his or her child at a key moment, such as at graduation or a sixteenth birthday. These words could reflect the love of God and biblical promises, or they could especially focus on the gifts and strengths of the young adult. Either way, this is something that should be reinstated if only because of the precious memories it would create for everyone involved. The grandparent would feel valued because he or she is given the time and space to breathe life into the future of the next generation by speaking specific words of hope. The parents would feel the tenderness and love from their parents for their children, and a link of intergenerational love would be established. Most of all, the experience could be formative for the children, guiding and encouraging them in dark times. Beyond the genuine care that would be demonstrated through it, a grandparent's blessing would simultaneously bestow to the grandchildren a sense of destiny and sense of their history—a sense of destiny because the grandchildren could hope to live up to the vision of their grandparents, and a sense of history because they would be connected with previous generations through these blessings.

So it was with Jacob. After an incredibly painful separation from Joseph, Jacob was miraculously rejoined with his lost son who had ascended to a position of great power within the Egyptian kingdom. Jacob had a short time before his death to reestablish a loving connection with Joseph and even had the privilege of building relationships with his grandchildren Ephraim and Manasseh. Out of these relationships, he was able to speak words of wisdom and prophecy to them both (see Genesis 48:15–16). After giving special attention to Ephraim and Manasseh, Jacob later spoke blessings over each of his children (see Genesis 49). By taking the time to bless his children and some of his grandchildren, Jacob was able to be a source of comfort and encouragement to his family during his final days.

We have the opportunity to project God into our familial relationships, and there's no reason to wait until we are at the end of our lives. We can speak words of life, hope, encouragement, and wisdom to our children, grandchildren, and other family members today. Jacob chose to wait until he was near death as a sort of parting blessing, but you can do this in any season. Whether occurring over dinner, during the natural rhythms of your day, or at a special event, a time set aside to bless your children or grandchildren can be encouraging and uplifting for everyone involved. It doesn't take a special event at all, just the presence of your family and a thoughtful spirit.

Jacob likely didn't come up with the blessings for his children and grandchildren on the spur of the moment. No, he spent some time considering the nature and character of each of his family members, their history with him, and those things he wanted to see develop in them. It will take us time to develop words of blessing too, but we can start today. Write down the names of the family members you'd like to bless and prayerfully consider who they are. What might God want to say to them when He could use you as a mouthpiece? What blessings do you wish to impart to each of them? Don't be afraid of overstepping boundaries, because, in this dark world, people are usually open to receiving kind words of encouragement.

_____

_____

_____

_____

_____

_____

_____

_____

_____

_____

_____

_____

_____

*Jesus, show me Your heart for my family
members that I might—like Jacob and
Isaac—offer a blessing to them. Amen.*

BLESSING

May you see the heart of God for your family. May you have the courage to share that heart with them. May your blessings be received with gladness and joy.

19

JOSEPH BELIEVED GOD WOULD RESCUE ISRAEL FROM EGYPT

It was by faith that Joseph, when he was about
to die, said confidently that the people of Israel
would leave Egypt. He even commanded them
to take his bones with them when they left.

HEBREWS 11:22

*Dear Jesus, teach me to have the boldness and
confidence of Joseph about Your promises.*

"Soon I will die," Joseph told his brothers, "but God
will surely come to help you and lead you out of this
land of Egypt. He will bring you back to the land he
solemnly promised to give to Abraham, to Isaac, and to
Jacob." Then Joseph made the sons of Israel swear an
oath, and he said, "When God comes to help you and
lead you back, you must take my bones with you."

GENESIS 50:24–25

Joseph experienced a lot of turmoil in his life but
never forgot the core promises of God to His people.
When his brothers sold him into slavery and he became a
servant at Potiphar's house, he kept in mind the reality that
God was with him. When he was wrongfully accused and
imprisoned, he strengthened himself with the presence of

God's goodness in his life. When he stood before Pharaoh to give the interpretation of the ruler's mysterious dreams, Joseph never lost sight of who God Himself promised to be to his family. And on his deathbed, Joseph held firm to the promises of God. Those promises guided him through his entire life (see Genesis 37–50 for the story of Joseph's life).

Joseph even staked his life upon the promise given by God to Abraham—that Israel would eventually be led out of Egypt and back into Canaan to receive its inheritance (see Genesis 15:16). As the second-in-command of all of Egypt, he had the right to a grand funeral procession. If you read about the death of Jacob, you can get a sense of the pomp and circumstance that could have accompanied Joseph's death. The people of Egypt mourned Jacob's death for seventy days, and then all the senior members of Pharaoh's household and his officials followed Joseph and his brothers back to bury Jacob in Canaan (Genesis 50:1–14). If all this was done to honor Joseph's father, we can only imagine what it would have looked like for Joseph himself. Yet instead of all this, Joseph made a simple request: hold my bones until Israel leaves Egypt. His confidence extended even to his death.

As in Joseph's case, our lives often appear as if God's promises are empty. For Joseph, his family had just left Canaan—where they did not own the land—and moved to Egypt at the request of the pharaoh. There was no clear path to the fulfillment of God's promised land for the Israelites, but Joseph hoped in this promise anyway. We have the same opportunity to place our faith in God's promises, even though nothing might be on the horizon to indicate God is at work. Like Joseph, we can place our confidence in the good character of our God instead of the story our circumstances tell us. It's a moment-by-moment decision, but nevertheless, we can cling to God.

It's time to stir some faith in your life by looking at a specific promise of God. Romans 8:31 says, "If God is for us, who can ever be against us?" Start by writing this verse at the top of your reflections for the day. Next, write your response to the following questions: What does it mean that God is "on your team"? Does it feel as if He is actively working on your behalf? What would it look like for you to choose courageously, as Joseph did—to place your faith in the good character of God and in His limitless ability to fulfill His promises, even when it seems as if there's no path to victory?

_____

_____

_____

_____

_____

_____

_____

_____

_____

_____

_____

_____

_____

_____

_____

_____

_____

_____

_____

_____

_____

_____

_____

*Jesus, give me the faith of Joseph, to trust You
in the dark when nothing makes sense. Amen.*

BLESSING

May you find strength in the story of Joseph. May you
fully trust that God is indeed for you. May you grow
into a faith that believes God is on your team, even when
your current circumstances seem to contradict that truth.

20

MOSES'S PARENTS HID HIM FROM PHARAOH

It was by faith that Moses' parents hid him for three months when he was born. They saw that God has given them an unusual child, and they were not afraid to disobey the king's command.

HEBREWS 11:23

Dear Jesus, I know You have called me out as Your own possession. Help me to understand what that means for me, today, right now.

Live clean, innocent lives as children of God, shining like bright lights in a world full of crooked and perverse people.

PHILIPPIANS 2:15

Moses's parents are never named in his initial birth story. Instead, we have to wait until the genealogies of Israel are listed several chapters later to learn that his father is Amram and his mother is Jochebed (Exodus 6:20). Still, these as-of-yet unnamed parents have a tremendous decision to make. They have a deep love for Moses, and this forces a decision upon them (see Exodus 2). Pharaoh commanded that every Hebrew boy must be killed as a wicked form of population control. Amram and Jochebed can't bring themselves to allow such a terrible thing to happen to their little boy. What are they to do, disobey the powers that be and risk imprisonment or worse? Or stand by and let their child be killed? The Exodus story tells us that Jochebed made the fateful decision to hide Moses from everyone for three months.

God redeems Jochebed's decision a few short months later. When Moses can no longer be hidden, she decides to set him adrift in the Nile River. Pharaoh's daughter finds Moses in the river while bathing and decides to take him as her own. She cannot nurse Moses, so she calls for a Hebrew nursing maid, and who else but Jochebed is called upon to nurse her own baby? Moses's mother is paid to care for Moses, and a beautiful season begins. Not only is Jochebed reunited with the child she might have never seen again when she launched Moses into the river, but she is also able to provide financially for her family in the process. Thus the goodness of God is demonstrated in this amazing moment. Yet Jochebed likely had unanswered questions. For example, why had God protected Moses when many other babies were being tossed into the Nile River to die?

While most of us will not experience the oppression and injustice Jochebed and her people did, nobody is immune from difficult decisions and seasons in life. We might feel prompted by the Holy Spirit to make a choice motivated by faith. And then we wait . . . and wait . . . and wait, but nothing happens. There is no miracle, there is no call to ministry, and there is no season of incredible blessing from God. Life just seems to go on as it always has, as though that decision never even happened. As I'm sure Jochebed did, we are left to question whether we even heard God right in the first place. And yet we know that there is a reason for the choice we made through His guidance, even though it might not make sense now. Here is the bottom line: We can trust that God is calling us to a life of showing His goodness. We can know that He has called us out of darkness into His wonderful light to draw others to this same hope. We can step forward in both faith and a bit of uncertainty, knowing that God will have our backs.

Write down Philippians 2:15: "Live clean, innocent lives as children of God, shining like bright lights in a world full of crooked and perverse people." What would it look like for you to shine like a "bright light" in a world of darkness? Maybe there is a better question for you: when is the last time someone asked about why you live life differently, and what does that say about the way you are living your life? Commit in a fresh new way to living a hope-filled life like Amram and Jochebed, even when the reasons don't fully make sense today.

_____

_____

_____

_____

_____

_____

_____

_____

_____

_____

_____

_____

_____

_____

_____

_____

_____

Jesus, I confess You are the reason for my hope, even though maybe it hasn't looked like it lately. I want to live in such a way that people are drawn to my Hope. Amen.

BLESSING

May you see in a fresh way that God has called you His own inheritance. May you be motivated to shine the light of God into a dark world. May you have opportunities to explain your hope.

21

MOSES FLED FROM SIN

It was by faith that Moses, when he grew up,
refused to be called the son of Pharaoh's daughter.
He chose to share the oppression of God's people
instead of enjoying the fleeting pleasures of sin.

HEBREWS 11:24–25

*Dear Jesus, give me a heart like Moses that doesn't
shy away from difficult circumstances but does
avoid the harmful and addictive habits of sin.*

You must have the same attitude that Christ
Jesus had.

Though he was God,
    he did not think of equality with God
    as something to cling to.
Instead, he gave up his divine privileges;
    he took the humble position of a slave
    and was born as a human being.
When he appeared in human form,
    he humbled himself in obedience to God
    and died a criminal's death on a cross.

PHILIPPIANS 2:5–8

There's a great scene at the beginning of the movie
The Prince of Egypt where Moses and the future Pharaoh are young men competing against each other. They are racing chariots through the streets of an Egyptian

city, creating havoc wherever they go as only the young can do. They fly up construction sites and scare people left and right. It makes for a great opening to a movie and really captures the audience's attention. Too bad the book of Hebrews never recorded such a race. While *The Prince of Egypt* was never meant to be an exact retelling of the Bible, one of the biggest alterations is this—in *The Prince of Egypt*, Moses was raised thinking he was an Egyptian and only finds out through a dream that he is not. Instead, we find Moses aware of his Hebraic roots and choosing to align himself with his people. In Hebrews 11, we read that "[Moses] refused to be called the son of Pharaoh's daughter. He chose to share the oppression of God's people" (vv. 24–25). In making this choice, Moses became a forerunner of what Jesus did for us.

Jesus left the accolades of heaven and became a human being. But He didn't come down as some majestic ruler to share wisdom from on high with the lowly people of Earth. No, He came as a baby boy to a poor family and lived as a nobody for thirty years. Then Jesus started His ministry, where He was consistently affiliating Himself with the poor, the unwanted, and the despised of His time. Then after living His life without a single sin, He died upon the cross to restore us to our relationship with God the Father. Jesus could have had anything He wanted, but He chose death because of His love for us. Jesus could have established an earthly kingdom that He was reigning over to this day, but He chose the humble path of obedience and humility.

We have the same choice before us every day, to step toward sin or to humbly submit ourselves to a life of purity under God's protection. Living this lifestyle will cost us something. Remember it cost Moses the luxuries of ancient Egypt, and it cost Jesus His very life. We must trust that the God who led Moses out of Egypt and to the very edge of the promised land, the same God who raised Jesus from the grave to declare victory over death, will work in our lives to accomplish His purposes as well.

Some days it's hard to live a Jesus-centered life. The draw of the things around us is just so strong. What challenges you to step away from Jesus's call to a life submitted to God? Write down the sins that you battle on a regular basis. Maybe you find that you compare yourself to others and desire their successes, or maybe you let your anger cause you to erupt in fits of rage. Perhaps you struggle with gossip or with using derogatory language or with lust. Whatever your battles are, record them in as much or as little detail as you want. These words are only for you and God to see, so you can write openly and honestly.

_____

_____

_____

_____

_____

_____

_____

Once you've written about your struggles, pray the prayer below as a first step toward victory over any recurring sin.

*Almighty God, I want to be like Moses
and Jesus who both stepped away from
temptation to honor You with their lives,
but if I'm honest, it's a real struggle right
now. I can't seem to let go of this problem,
no matter how hard I try. I need Your
strength to overcome it. Would You come and
empower me to live more purely? Amen.*

BLESSING

May you be encouraged by the example of Moses who stepped away from luxury to find his calling in life. May you know what it means to be free of condemnation and judgment over your mistakes. May you walk in victory over sin.

22

MOSES UNDERSTOOD HIS REWARD

He [Moses] thought it was better to suffer for the
sake of Christ than to own the treasures of Egypt,
for he was looking ahead to his great reward.

HEBREWS 11:26

*Dear Jesus, I long to understand the reward that I
will receive at the end of this life of serving You.*

Dear friends, we are already God's children, but
he has not yet shown us what we will be like when
Christ appears. But we do know that we will be
like him, for we will see him as he really is.

1 JOHN 3:2

Moses kept his eyes on the prize. For Moses, "the
prize" was to enter the land of Canaan. While Moses
was still in the wilderness of Midian, God came to him
and told him that he—Moses—had been chosen to lead
the Israelites from Egypt into a land flowing with milk
and honey (Exodus 3–4).

Sadly, Moses did not enter the promised land. After
courageously standing up to Pharaoh and intrepidly
leading the people out of Egypt, Moses then allowed
his anger to get the best of him, and he misrepresented
the heart of God to Israel when he gave them water in

the wilderness (see Numbers 20:7–12). Instead, he was granted the privilege of seeing the promised land only from the top of Mount Nebo, and then he died. In an interesting turn of events, Moses posthumously stepped foot in the land promised to Israel. At the transfiguration of Jesus, the disciples see Jesus with Moses and Elijah and are essentially dumbfounded. This means God, in His kindness, allowed Moses to step foot in the promised land after all!

We have a somewhat mysterious promise of future blessings provided for us in Christ. Even the apostle John stated that we don't know exactly what happens when Jesus returns, but that it's something momentous and life-altering (1 John 3:2). John said, "We will be like him," because we will see Him in all His glory, but what does that mean? It is a mystery, but one we can believe. When we are struggling to make sense of our circumstances, we can hold fast to the fact that all will be different on the other side of eternity. It might feel like a small reward considering the struggles we are having right now, but let's remember that the apostle Paul said our momentary afflictions are nothing compared to the glory that will be revealed in us (Romans 8:18). And when Paul talked about momentary afflictions, he was including things like being stoned, shipwrecked, and tortured—still he said it was nothing compared to our future in Christ.

We often live very small-mindedly, focused on the things that aren't going well and exaggerating their importance in the overall scheme of things. Because we don't have a sense of the grander things happening in the world and the universe, we are sometimes like the teenager who says her life is over because her boyfriend broke up with her. Our universes are smaller than they could be, and we risk losing out on some of the blessings God has in store for us. Like Moses, we might end up on the outside looking in on our own promised land.

What small thing have you been exaggerating in your life, in terms of how important it is? (Mind you, this is not the time to say that, for example, being unemployed is a small thing—we're talking about inconveniences that we treat as life-ending events.) Name this small thing. Journal a little about why it's felt too large in your life and how you'd like its impact to be smaller starting today.

_____

_____

_____

_____

_____

_____

_____

_____

_____

_____

_____

_____

*Jesus, give me a longer view of the struggles
I'm having in my life, so they don't feel as
overwhelming as they do right now. Amen.*

BLESSING

May you get a vision for what our inheritance in Jesus
could look like. May your struggles be seen in light of
eternity. May your heart be encouraged to better manage
difficult times that will inevitably arise.

23

MOSES DIDN'T FEAR PHARAOH

It was by faith that Moses left the land of Egypt,
not fearing the king's anger. He kept right on going
because he kept his eyes on the one who is invisible.

HEBREWS 11:27

*Dear Jesus, help me, like Moses, keep my eyes on the
Father—the great unseen one who rules over all—and
not to fear things in this world that can harm me.*

All honor and glory to God forever and ever!
He is the eternal King, the unseen one who
never dies; he alone is God. Amen.

1 TIMOTHY 1:17

The heart of the Exodus story is remarkable. A single pair of brothers confront one of the most powerful rulers in the world at the time, and they make demands of him and threaten him. At any moment, Pharaoh could have had Moses and Aaron imprisoned or even killed, but this didn't stop them from continuing to come forward with requests and threats against the people and the land of Egypt. Instead, they remain steadfast in following the directions given to them by God, and the results are unbelievable. Not only did the Israelites leave Egypt safely, but they are given gold, gems, and other precious items by the Egyptians on the way out (Exodus 12:35–36). The text says that Israel "plundered" Egypt (v. 36 NIV). They found freedom from slavery by obeying God.

We don't have the same stakes in our lives. We are generally not threatened with death or imprisonment for obeying God. We aren't enslaved right now. But we can still allow the power of other people, circumstances, and structures to intimidate us and keep us from following God's best for our lives. We can be among those who shrink back and cower in fear instead of pushing forward in hard obedience. The key to overcoming this fear is to remember who exactly has the true power in every situation. God alone is King. Only He has authority in the circumstances of our lives.

We must hold fast to the idea that God is in charge and allow that concept to empower us to overcome fear.

We all have circumstances or people that intimidate us. Maybe it's your boss's boss or your loud aunt, or maybe it's looking at your budget every month. Our human tendency is to actively avoid things that intimidate us, but often that just gets us into more trouble. We must learn to step forward in spite of fear and face that person or thing that intimidates us.

Write out who or what it is that intimidates you and makes you feel small. Then write this prayer:

> *God, You are God even over this. I*
> *give [person, stressor, or circumstance]*
> *to You, and commit to following You*
> *through this, no matter what.*

_____

_____

_____

_____

_____

_____

_____

_____

_____

_____

_____

_____

_____

For today's prayer you can use the prayer you just wrote.

BLESSING

May you find undiscovered courage as you obey God. May you see the length and breadth of the power of God. In your obedience, may you rest in the abundance that your Father offers.

24

ISRAEL AND THE RED SEA

It was by faith that the people of Israel went
right through the Red Sea as though they
were on dry ground. But when the Egyptians
tried to follow, they were all drowned.

HEBREWS 11:29

*Dear Jesus, flex Your strength in my life that
I might recall the grandeur of Your might.
Help me to never take You for granted.*

Wake up, wake up, O LORD! Clothe yourself
    with strength!
    Flex your mighty right arm!
Rouse yourself as in the days of old
    when you slew Egypt, the dragon of the
        Nile.
Are you not the same today,
    the one who dried up the sea,
making a path of escape through the depths
    so that your people could cross over?

ISAIAH 51:9–10

Some verses almost argue with each other. The jux-
taposition between today's two featured passages is
remarkable. In the first verse, Hebrews 11:29, the victory
of God is ready and evident for all to see. This verse represents the Israelites' experience when the Red Sea parted.
The Israelites were keenly aware of the active presence of

God and His victory on their behalf. There was no question as to whether God was for Israel because the answer was obvious.

In Isaiah 51:9–10, this victory at the Red Sea is a vague memory dulled by the difficulties of a present life without the grand majesty of God. The Isaiah verses are nearly accusatory, the author wondering whether God is still capable of performing miracles for Israel. The prophet cries out for God to wake up, to gird himself with strength, and to act on behalf of the nation (v. 9). He questions whether God has changed or if He is still the same God of the old stories.

In our own lives, we can waver between these two postures toward God. When the victories of God are recent and obvious, we can state as a fact that God is for us, and we can trust in Him inherently because of His power. But when the victories are in the past and times are rough, it's far too easy to relegate the victories of God to only the past. We can join Isaiah and wonder if God has somehow changed His tune or His stance toward us. Though Romans 8:31 promises God is for us, we can be left questioning if that's the case when we experience trials and hardships.

In these moments we can find comfort in the knowledge that we have permission to join Isaiah in his lament calling God to rise up on our behalf. There is no shame and no sin in asking God where He is, reminding Him of His amazing provision and protection over the years, and pondering aloud why God isn't showing up. He can handle our questions, He knows our weaknesses, and He expects us to be honest with Him. If we are in a dark season, it's okay to ask God to bring light to pierce the night.

Are the victories of God clear and evident in your life, or are you wondering when God is going to show up as the righteous king in your calamities? It's important to take stock of your circumstances because, to a certain degree, they influence our relationship with God. We must be transparent with ourselves and with God, but sometimes this is difficult. Once you've identified your posture toward God, recount in as much detail as possible your favorite "God moment" in your life. When did you experience God as real and present and on your side? Make that memory your own "Red Sea moment." You can choose to revisit this personal Red Sea moment in the same way that Israel was always returning to the memory of the Red Sea crossing.

_____

_____

_____

_____

_____

_____

_____

_____

_____

_____

*Jesus, restore my faith in Your goodness
if I'm in a rough spot, and prepare
me for those future rough spots if
I'm flourishing today. Amen.*

BLESSING

May you recognize the constancy of God's goodness toward you. May you be filled with joy as you consider your personal Red Sea moment. May your faith awaken and grow by remembering your personal experience of God's victory in your life. May your "God moment" become the knot at the end of your faith rope to which you can cling, whatever your external circumstances.

25

THE WALLS OF JERICHO TUMBLED DOWN

It was by faith that the people of Israel
marched around Jericho for seven days,
and the walls came crashing down.

HEBREWS 11:30

*Dear Jesus, move me past the familiarity of
the Jericho story and fill me with a fresh sense
of wonder and a belief that whatever You call
me to do can and will be accomplished.*

The LORD will march forth like a mighty hero; he
will come out like a warrior, full of fury. He will
shout his battle cry and crush all his enemies.

ISAIAH 42:13

Imagine being told to attack an enemy by going on a
power walk and intermittently playing an instrument.
That's the odd military strategy God presented to Israel
to conquer Jericho (Joshua 6). Let's take a moment to
recenter on the story as it actually took place. Israel had
just entered the promised land after wandering for a generation in the wilderness, and they were anxious to begin
receiving their inheritance. Then the direction of God
came to Joshua through the Angel of the Lord, and the
instructions were . . . well, they were weird and not like

the previous military commands given from the Lord. Previously God had commanded the Israelites to conquer the lands on the other side of the Jordan by going into battle just like any other army. And victory had come quickly. But this time, Israel is told to march around the city once a day for six days with the ark of the covenant (Joshua 6:2–5). Nothing else, just march around the city once. Then on the seventh day, they are to walk around the city seven times and, following that exercise, blow their trumpets. According to God, this was the path to victory.

Rather than skimming through this story because of its familiarity, dwell on it for just a moment with me, to make it more real. Israel had a large army and was perhaps itching to conquer something, and they were told to march around the city with the ark of the covenant for a bunch of days, then to blow their trumpets. This sounds downright silly. What possible reason would the Angel of the Lord have for giving such a ridiculous set of commands? The reason is found in today's verse, Isaiah 42:13. God wanted to show that He is the true source of power, that He is the true rescuer, that He is the warrior for the nation of Israel. He wanted to remind them that He was their source of strength and what differentiated them from other nations. It is because Israel was God's chosen people that they were able to conquer the land of Canaan, not because of their own military prowess. God was unapologetically on their side.

It is the same with us today. First Peter calls us a holy, chosen nation of priests (1 Peter 2:9). There are moments in our lives where God calls us to step back and watch Him move in remarkable ways. This can be very difficult and can cause confusion, because it seems as if we are doing nothing when we ought to act. It can even lead to a season of darkness as we wait on God, because His timing is often very different than ours. And this is the very point: God wants to coach us in patience (see Galatians 5:22–23) and remind us that He is a warrior on our behalf (see Exodus 15:3).

Many of us find ourselves in a situation right now where God is directing us to wait with expectation for His movement in our lives. This can be frustrating, especially in today's world that values action and movement. We want to take control of the situation, but the Lord tells us to walk around the city and blow a trumpet (Joshua 6:4). It can be infuriating. Whether that's your circumstance today or not, there is value in remembering the battles that God has won on your behalf.

Write down the answer to this question: When did God win a battle on your behalf that would have been an impossible victory in your own strength? Allow the memory of this moment to run through your spiritual veins as if it happened yesterday and to stir your faith in the goodness and capability of God, even if you're in the darkness and waiting today.

_____

_____

_____

_____

_____

_____

_____

_____

_____

_____

_____

_____

_____

Jesus, even in the darkness of waiting, I trust
You to be a warrior on my behalf. Amen.

BLESSING

May you clearly hear when God tells you to walk around your Jericho instead of entering directly into battle. May you learn to honor God as a warrior on your behalf. May you see the victory in your life that God has promised (Romans 8:37).

26

RAHAB WAS MORE THAN A PROSTITUTE

It was by faith that Rahab the prostitute
was not destroyed with the people in her
city who refused to obey God. For she had
given a friendly welcome to the spies.

HEBREWS 11:31

*Dear Jesus, teach me to view myself redemptively
instead of by my past choices and actions.*

I will also bless the foreigners who commit themselves
to the LORD, who serve him and love his name, who
worship him and do not desecrate the Sabbath day of
rest, and who hold fast to my covenant. I will bring
them to my holy mountain of Jerusalem and will fill
them with joy in my house of prayer. I will accept
their burnt offerings and sacrifices, because my Temple
will be called a house of prayer for all nations.

ISAIAH 56:6—7

Rahab gets an unfortunate rap. In the book of Hebrews, she is called "Rahab the prostitute" (v. 31).
Although the focus of her story in the Bible is on her extraordinary faith, we sadly often remember her only by
her profession. As we piece together the various threads

of Rahab's narrative from the Bible, we discover there is much more to her story.

First, she protected two spies that Joshua sent into Jericho. To these two strange, foreign men, she showed kindness by letting them stay at her house for the evening and then hiding them when the king sent men to capture those spies. She even gave the spies sage advice to successfully go into hiding to avoid being detected as she helped them escape.

But what she said in her conversation with the spies before she sent them safely away is the beginning of her redemption (Joshua 2:8–14). She professed faith in God as the maker of heaven and Earth and declared faith that God has given Canaan into the hands of Israel. Because she believed that Israel was going to conquer Jericho and because she helped save the spies' lives, Rahab asked them for protection for herself and her family.

Rahab and her family were provided safety by the advancing army of Israel after the capture of Jericho, and Rahab joined the nation of Israel. This isn't directly indicated in the Joshua narrative, but we pick up the last piece of Rahab's story in the New Testament when we see her name included in Jesus's genealogy (Matthew 1:5). Rahab married Salmon from the tribe of Judah and lived a faithful life, from everything the Scriptures tell us. Her rescue from Jericho was the beginning of a retelling of her story, and she made the most of her opportunity to recast her life.

Maybe like Rahab you feel branded by your past. Perhaps you feel like there is too much shame in your history for God to ever use you or truly even love you. Take heart, friend—nothing you have done or will do can disqualify you from God and His love. The ultimate sacrifice by Jesus on the cross paved the way for you to enter a fresh relationship with God based on Christ's merits, not your own. Like Rahab, you have been brought into a new family and you have the privilege of building a new history.

Writing down our thoughts allows us to pay special attention to what we are doing.

Doing so can even rewire our brain. Let's use this exercise to rewire our brain right now! Too often we believe that we are disqualified from great service to God because of something we've done in our past. But that's not the story of Scripture. Write down 2 Corinthians 5:17 from the New International Version of the Bible: "If anyone is in Christ, the new creation has come: The old has gone, the new is here!" Okay, now underneath the verse, record all the reasons you feel as if God might disqualify you, and then ask God to help you let those beliefs go in light of your new identity. While rewiring our brain's pathways involves choices made over time, declaring to ourselves that we are new creations in Christ can begin replacing those false narratives with the amazing truth of our redeemed, free, and whole identity in God.

_____

_____

_____

_____

_____

_____

_____

_____

_____

_____

_____

*Jesus, I want to believe I am a new
creation, but it's often hard to let go
of the old narratives—give me faith
to believe Your Bible. Amen.*

BLESSING

May you recognize that your past does not define your future in Jesus. May you let go of the old habits that used to define you. May you grab hold of a new vision and destiny for yourself in Christ.

27

GIDEON STILL HAD FAITH

How much more do I need to say? It would take too
long to recount the stories of the faith of Gideon, Barak,
Samson, Jephthah, David, Samuel, and all the prophets.

HEBREWS 11:32

Dear Jesus, teach me to be patient with myself
as I work through my current circumstances
in light of the call of God on my life.

Gideon son of Joash was threshing wheat at the
bottom of a winepress to hide the grain from the
Midianites. The angel of the LORD appeared to him
and said, "Mighty hero, the LORD is with you!"
"Sir," Gideon replied, "if the LORD is with us, why
has all this happened to us? And where are all the
miracles our ancestors told us about? Didn't they say,
'The LORD brought us up out of Egypt'? But now
the LORD has abandoned us and handed us over to
the Midianites." Then the LORD turned to him and
said, "Go with the strength you have, and rescue
Israel from the Midianites. I am sending you!"

JUDGES 6:11–14

Gideon gets the short end of the stick in our memories. We are quick to make light of him for asking
God for proof that He was with Gideon and was going
to grant him military success. This ignores the miserable
plight of the nation of Israel from the oppression of the

Midianites. The Midianites' control wasn't just domination—the Bible tells us the Israelites were starving because the Midianites demanded all their food sources. This was a severe situation, and an unsuccessful Israelite uprising not only would make matters worse for Israel but would probably result in Gideon's own death. Gideon was being reasonable when he was looking for evidence of God's guidance and protection.

It was out of this sense of desperation and frustration that Gideon asked the Angel of the Lord why Israel was in such turmoil if God was with him. He recounted the great deeds of the past and pointed out that these deeds were far removed from his present circumstances. It's important to note what didn't happen when Gideon made these statements and accused God of abandoning Israel to Midian. The Angel of the Lord didn't jump down his throat, He didn't accuse him of lacking faith, and He didn't have any anger. Instead, He reiterated His call on Gideon's life. He told Gideon to rescue Israel in the strength he had and said that he was being sent by God. And here's the important thing: even though Gideon put God through a series of other faith tests, at the end of the day, he did exactly what God called him to. He rescued Israel from Midian with some remarkable military victories.

We can fall into the trap of judging ourselves for being honest with God about our circumstances. We can feel as though the only way to respond to God is with absolute faith every time and every day, even though that's not the pattern we see in the Bible. It is okay to be frustrated and lack faith in the goodness of God because we're dwelling in a dark place. God won't be offended, but He also won't change His calling on our lives. As God did with

Gideon, He will listen to our complaints and still send us out. God can handle our questions. Ultimately, God is more concerned with our obedience than with the honest questions we have before we begin to obey.

Take time to answer these questions: Is God calling you to do something specific right now? What objections do you have about this thing God is calling you to do?

After you are done writing, bring these concerns to God in prayer. Now sit in stillness for at least two minutes and listen carefully for the Holy Spirit to speak to you about your worries. Don't worry if this is new or uncomfortable or if you don't sense His direction this time around. However, listen with expectation that God will speak. Know this: God longs to meet with you more than you desire to meet with Him. Write down what you sense the Holy Spirit is saying as you wait upon Him.

_____

_____

_____

_____

_____

_____

_____

_____

_____

_____

_____

_____

*Jesus, I let go of my fear about whatever
You might be calling me to in this moment,
and I commit to following You. Amen.*

BLESSING

May you learn the blessing of questioning God. May you begin to see that He is not so fragile that you can't ask Him questions. May you grow in your obedience toward God.

28

BARAK PUT CONDITIONS ON HIS FAITH

How much more do I need to say? It would take too long to recount the stories of the faith of Gideon, Barak, Samson, Jephthah, David, Samuel, and all the prophets.

HEBREWS 11:32

Dear Jesus, teach me to be obedient
to You without conditions.

Barak told her, "I will go, but only if you go with me." "Very well," she replied, "I will go with you. But you will receive no honor in this venture, for the LORD's victory over Sisera will be at the hands of a woman." So Deborah went with Barak to Kedesh.

JUDGES 4:8–9

Barak is a fascinating study of faith and fear. Barak was called by the judge and prophetess Deborah to defeat Israelite's oppressors—the Canaanites—in battle (see Judges 4–5 for the whole story). He was willing to lead his people to victory, but with conditions.

Apparently, he didn't have enough faith to believe that God would go with him unless Deborah joined him. Deborah did go with him, but the decision to include Deborah had consequences for Barak. The ultimate victory over the Canaanite commander Sisera was taken from him and given to a woman named Jael. In one of the more grotesque narratives of Scripture, Jael hammers a tent peg through Sisera's temple to kill him after giving him a drink and soothing him to sleep. Instead of dying in battle with Barak, Sisera is killed while hiding from the Israelite army and Barak. The songs that are sung about Deborah and Barak then include giving honor to Jael as the ultimate victor over Sisera, an honor that seemingly would have gone to Barak if his faith had been stronger.

Barak is an interesting contrast with yesterday's judge, Gideon. While Gideon questioned God, he ultimately obeyed everything God called him to do. Barak, in contrast, needed to put a condition on his obedience. That is why the honor was stripped from Barak and not from Gideon. While Barak was entrusted with a difficult task, he should have been able to trust that Deborah was hearing from God, because she was both prophetess and judge, given dual responsibilities by God to hear from God for the people of Israel. Instead, Barak thought he needed her presence with him to guarantee the victory because he deemed the direction from God insufficient to trust.

We can fall into the same problem if we aren't careful. We can put conditions on our obedience to God instead of trusting Him fully. For example, we can say that we will show practical love to someone if they are kind to us first, or that we will be generous with our finances only if we have extra cash at the end of the month. Both examples follow the pattern of Barak, where fear trumps obedience, causing our faith to fall flat.

It's time for a heart and gut check. Consider the following question: Where are you allowing fear to keep you from obeying fully? We all have areas where this is true; remember that there is no condemnation for those in Christ, but let's address those areas now. In a prayer to God, write down where you are struggling to follow Him in faith, and commit yourself to quick and complete obedience when God calls you to do something.

_____

_____

_____

_____

_____

_____

_____

_____

_____

_____

_____

_____

Jesus, increase my faith so that I don't falter like Barak did and lose opportunities for victories in my life. Amen.

BLESSING

May you learn from the example of Barak and not shrink back from opportunities to lead. May you distinguish between the posture of going before God with all your fears and questions, as Gideon did, and one of disobedience, as Barak demonstrated. May your faith call you to obedience even when it's scary.

29

JEPHTHAH LED WITH LOGIC AND PEACE

How much more do I need to say? It would take too long to recount the stories of the faith of Gideon, Barak, Samson, Jephthah, David, Samuel, and all the prophets.

HEBREWS 11:32

Dear Jesus, remind me that faith and reason are not separate entities, but that they work together.

Then Jephthah sent messengers to the king of Ammon, asking "Why have you come out to fight against my land?"

JUDGES 11:12

Jephthah was a very thoughtful man. You can read many times in his story in Judges 11–12 that he always seemed to lead with reason, yet he is included in the Hebrews "Hall of Faith." This is a fascinating dynamic, one worth considering, because some people think faith and reason are diametrically opposed.

In Judges 11–12, Jephthah was trying to avoid war with Ammon. Jephthah started the conversation with the question, "Why have you come out to fight against my land?" The king of Ammon replied that Israel had stolen land the people of Ammon had historically claimed as theirs. Jephthah responded with a historical account of how Israel conquered the land of the Amorites after they refused to allow the Israelites to pass through the land unscathed. Then he ended with a challenge to the king—to keep whatever land their god Chemosh gave them and to leave Israel alone. The king of Ammon ignored Jephthah, and the war continued. It is noteworthy that Jephthah led with reason rather than leading with war. Many military leaders are presumed to lead with force, but Jephthah didn't follow this expected pattern.

After Jephthah's victory over Ammon, the people of Ephraim threatened to burn down his house because he didn't include them in the call to arms. Faithful to his pattern, Jephthah led with logic and recounted what actually happened. He called Ephraim to support his war against Ammon, but Ephraim did not respond. Then Jephthah again asked a question—why do you want to fight me now? As happened with Ammon, Jephthah's diplomacy was stonewalled. He went to war against Ephraim and was victorious a second time.

Jephthah is a very relatable hero in Scripture. He doesn't seem to lead with grand acts of faith or perform miraculous deeds like some of the other heroes in the Bible. Instead, he led with logic and diplomacy first. When these tactics weren't successful, he then moved to military action, but only after peace had failed. Jephthah's leadership, as demonstrated in Judges 11–12, can challenge us in two ways. First, are we allowing space in our lives for logic to lead the way, even in issues of faith? Sometimes logic is a perfectly appropriate response. We've been conditioned to think that we have to muster up spiritual faith to move forward in a decision, but there are seasons where it's completely appropriate and helpful to lead with logic. After all, God did give us our brain and our spirit, right?

The second challenge to us from the life of Jephthah is how he often led with peace. While Jephthah used logic to achieve his goals, his intention was to avoid arguments or, in his case, war. He wanted to resolve disagreements as peaceably as possible. Often in our lives, we want to lead with argumentation or division. We don't see a path to victory, so we dig in our heels and get ready to go to proverbial war. Jephthah shows us there is a better way, a peaceable way.

Of these two disciplines—leading with logic or prioritizing peace—one may present a bigger challenge to you. Perhaps you were raised in a church that spiritualized everything, and it feels ungodly to lean into logic for direction or guidance. Let me remind you again that God gave you the brain in your head as much as he did your spirit, and it's unwise to ignore it. On the flip side, maybe it is leading with peace instead of a sword that is your Achilles' heel. You might be used to arguing your way to victory or using emotion to manipulate people into giving you your way. Neither of these honor God. Jesus is known as the Prince of Peace, after all.

Write down whether you struggle more with trusting logic or prioritizing peace. Outline why you have a hard time with the discipline you chose. Ask the Lord to give you the next right step.

_____

_____

_____

_____

Jesus, help me to lead like Jephthah, who wasn't afraid to lean into his logic or to lead with peace, even when it seemed as if war was imminent. Amen.

BLESSING

May you learn from this unlikely hero. May you use logic and diplomacy when it makes sense to do so. May you always start with peace, not war.

30

DAVID ANOINTED AS KING

How much more do I need to say? It would take too long to recount the stories of the faith of Gideon, Barak, Samson, Jephthah, David, Samuel, and all the prophets.

HEBREWS 11:32

Dear Jesus, there are things I've waited many years for that You've promised me. Continue to give me the patience to wait for Your timing.

So as David stood there among his brothers, Samuel took the flask of olive oil he had brought and anointed David with the oil. And the Spirit of the LORD came powerfully upon David from that day on.

1 SAMUEL 16:13

David's anointing altered the trajectory of his life. In a single moment, he went from being a shepherd to becoming the future king of Israel. He had been called in from taking care of his family's sheep only to be anointed Israel's shepherd by Samuel the prophet (1 Samuel 16:1–13). Surely this would usher immediate changes into David's life, and, surely, he would assume the duties and responsibilities of being the king right after this moment. Except that's not what happened. Instead, he waited over fifteen years before taking the throne of Israel. And the waiting was not a passive waiting. No, he had to constantly dodge the reigning King Saul and his anger and jealousy toward David.

The king was so angry that David would be his successor, David had to literally sidestep spears from Saul. One day David was playing a musical instrument to soothe Saul's mind. Instead of being soothed, the king became enraged and tried to pin David to the wall with a spear. The craziest thing is this: David had to go back to work as the king's musician the next day (1 Samuel 18:10–11)! Fastforward several years and David had proven himself as one of Saul's best warriors, consistently fighting and winning battles for the king. This stirred jealousy in Saul. His hostility was significant enough that David ascertained he needed to leave Israel, and that's what he did. That wasn't the end of the story, though. King Saul chased after him into the wilderness and into a cave in order to kill him outright. Don't worry; Saul didn't succeed.

David had to endure all these things and more after he was anointed as the next king of Israel. His life didn't get simpler; it got more difficult. Eventually, he did ascend to the throne, but only after many trials. The same can be true in our lives. We can have a sense of destiny from God and expect things to be simple and to become fun really quickly, but instead we find ourselves trying to dodge spears and hiding out in caves.

Some of us may have some specific promise that we believe God has given to us that we are waiting to lay hold of. Perhaps it is the salvation of a particular family member or maybe it's a call to full-time ministry. It could even be freedom from childhood trauma that still haunts you.

Instead of seeing any progress on your promise, you experience nothing but hindrances and frustration. Now is the time to let it all out. Write down your "David anointing" moment, the time you sensed God gave you this promise. After this specific promise was given to you, have you ever felt abandoned by God? Confess this and your frustration to God, and then sit in the quiet of that struggle for a few moments. Ask God to give you some guidance as to why there is a delay and wait to hear what He says. Write down His answer to you.

_____

_____

_____

_____

_____

_____

_____

_____

_____

_____

_____

_____

_____

Jesus, I confess I'm tired of waiting to
see the fulfillment of my dreams, but
I'm doing my best to hold on. Amen.

BLESSING

May you find joy in waiting for the fulfillment of God's promises. May you trust that God has not forgotten you no matter how your circumstances appear or how insignificant you feel. May you not lose heart as you wait.

31

DAVID WROTE OPENLY ABOUT HIS PAIN

How much more do I need to say? It would take too long to recount the stories of the faith of Gideon, Barak, Samson, Jephthah, David, Samuel, and all the prophets.

HEBREWS 11:32

Dear Jesus, I want to be as comfortable as David with expressing my pain and disappointment to You.

I am sick at heart.
How long, O LORD, until you restore me?

Return, O LORD, and rescue me.
Save me because of your unfailing love.

PSALM 6:3–4

Faith is not always represented as unfailing strength. Sometimes it shows up as weakness and transparency before the throne of our God. This is a common theme in the Old Testament, one that is too often forgotten. There is a long history of the people of God standing before Him, reminding Him of who He is and calling upon Him to act in accordance with His character. Abraham did this before God destroyed Sodom and Gomorrah. Moses did this after the nation of Israel formed the golden calf and worshiped it. And David does this all throughout the Psalms in what are called psalms of lament. Through these psalms, David cries out to God and asks for His help in desperation.

In Psalm 6, David says he is sick at heart and waiting on God to restore him and rescue him (vv. 2–3). But first, God must return to him, and David reminds God that this is something God should do because of His unfailing love (v. 4). Later in the psalm, he says that he is flooding his bed with tears and his vision is blinded by grief. David is overcome by the difficulty of his circumstances (vv. 6–7). Yet he ends this psalm with a declaration of faith, but even this is an interesting statement. David states with confidence that the Lord has heard his plea and will answer him (v. 9). He never says how God will answer his prayer, or that he will be rescued from his difficulties, even though that was his prayer. Instead, he takes confidence that God has heard his prayer.

Too often we are bereft of hope. We expect that God will rescue us from our problems, and we may even get angry when He doesn't. Yet we're invited to learn from David and take courage from the fact that the great Creator of the universe has heard our prayers. No matter how our circumstances appear at the time, let's put our hope in God's reliable, rock-solid character and in His tender-hearted, unfailing love for us: we can trust that He is the one who is always at work on our behalf. This is a different mentality though, one that relies upon the revealed nature of God to bless those He loves, rather than relying upon external evidence of God's good heart toward us.

Think back on a prayer that God never seemed to answer that was—or continues to be—particularly painful. Now consider the fruit of that unanswered prayer in your life. Record that specific prayer and the results of God's seeming silence. Though this could be an exercise in praise, it doesn't have to be. God allows heartaches into our lives for many reasons, and most of these struggles honestly don't make any sense in the moment or even in hindsight. Your unfulfilled prayer could still be a source of pain for you, and it might result in a lament-like psalm of your own toward God. Lament is a good and transparent interaction with God, and He honors radical honesty. (If this memory is triggering pain from your past, you have my permission to step back and stop this exercise, as we aren't trying to stir up old pain.) Given time, there's also a chance that you can see the intentions of God in this unanswered prayer. If that's the case, write this down as well. We have an opportunity to grow in our understanding of who God is and how He works in our lives.

_____

_____

_____

_____

_____

_____

_____

_____

_____

_____

_____

Jesus, I connect with David and his psalm
of lament some days, and I long to be
as honest with You as he was. Give me
the confidence to do just this. Amen.

BLESSING

May you become more comfortable talking to God about the areas of life that are uncomfortable, painful, or aggravating. May you see the unending generosity of God in your life as you look back on your answered and unanswered prayers. May you learn to trust in the character of God even when He seems absent.

32

DAVID CLAIMS A GREAT VICTORY FOR GOD

How much more do I need to say? It would take too long to recount the stories of the faith of Gideon, Barak, Samson, Jephthah, David, Samuel, and all the prophets.

HEBREWS 11:32

Dear Jesus, teach me to stand firm against enemies, confident in Your capacity to bring victory.

But David persisted. "I have been taking care of my father's sheep and goats," he said. "When a lion or a bear comes to steal a lamb from the flock, I go after it with a club and rescue the lamb from its mouth. If the animal turns on me, I catch it by the jaw and club it to death. I have done this to both lions and bears, and I'll do it to this pagan Philistine, too, for he has defied the armies of the living God! The LORD who rescued me from the claws of the lion and the bear will rescue me from this Philistine!"

1 SAMUEL 17:34–37

David had guts! In 1 Samuel 17:34–37, we pick up the story of David and Goliath right in the middle. David had just asked King Saul to allow him to fight Goliath, a Philistine giant intimidating the armies of Israel. Saul had told him it was an unreasonable request because David was a boy and Goliath a seasoned warrior. We see

David's response here, and it's worth meditating on for a moment. David was relying on God, but he was also relying on his past successes as a protector. Killing lions and bears by clubbing them to death is no small feat, so he had some experience of his own to lean into.

We can see, however, that he was fundamentally relying upon God to protect him. He looked at the fact that Goliath was defying the armies of God and expected God to "have his back" as he went out to battle on God's behalf. And this is precisely what God did—He delivered Goliath into David's hands. Though Goliath was armed with sword and spear and shield, David defeated him with a slingshot and a stone. David had earlier promised that he would cut off Goliath's head with his own sword (1 Samuel 17:46), and that's exactly what happened. He led Israel into a great victory, based both on his faith in his prior victories and, most of all, on his faith in God to protect the people of God from their enemies.

We have much to learn from David in this moment. Often Christians seem to believe that it is ungodly to view our own strengths or our own past as a reason to trust in the outcome of something in the future, but that is precisely what David did. We can do the same. We can look honestly at what we have accomplished in the past and trust that, in Christ's strength, we will perform similarly in the future. Of course, we must balance this with a confidence in God to work in and through us to accomplish a task. To rely fully and only on ourselves is a recipe for disaster, because God promises to humble the proud and exalt the lowly (James 4:10).

It can be particularly difficult when a "Goliath" is taunting us in our lives. We can feel ill-equipped to handle the tasks set before us because whatever the so-called

Goliath represents—whether financial strain or anxiety or stress—it is challenging us to come out and fight, but we don't seem to have the tools necessary for success. Perhaps we look at our Goliath's height, sword, spear, and shield, and then look at our slingshot and the stones we can pick up on the way to the battlefield, and we just feel inadequate. It's not always easy to rely on our past victories or to trust that God is going to help us fight our battles, because sometimes we see the enemy more clearly than we see God in our midst.

Who or what is the "Goliath" in your life right now? Maybe you don't have any Goliaths at this moment; if that's you, praise God for that, but know a giant is coming because that's how life works. If you know who or what your Goliath is, though, answer that question as honestly as you can. Describe what it is about this Goliath that makes it intimidating, and what has held you back from beginning to attack it. Now write out a prayer where you specifically ask God for courage, strength, and a strategy to overcome this Goliath using the twin tools of God-confidence and self-confidence. Wait for a few minutes to see if God answers your prayer with guidance or comfort or both and reflect on His response to you.

*Jesus, show me what it means to balance
confidence and humility as David did. Amen.*

BLESSING

May you gain a better view of your own skills and abilities. May you develop confidence in yourself. May you walk in humility before God so that He can exalt you.

33

SAMUEL'S MOTHER WAS BLESSED BY GOD

How much more do I need to say? It would take too long to recount the stories of the faith of Gideon, Barak, Samson, Jephthah, David, Samuel, and all the prophets.

HEBREWS 11:32

Dear Jesus, give me the courage to desperately ask You for the thing I want the most, and to subsequently be willing to give that thing right back to You in worship.

Hannah was in deep anguish, crying bitterly as she prayed to the LORD. And she made this vow: "O LORD of Heaven's Armies, if you will look upon my sorrow and answer my prayer and give me a son, then I will give him back to you. He will be yours for his entire lifetime."

1 SAMUEL 1:10–11

Hannah's path to motherhood wasn't easy. Hannah would become Samuel's mother, but only after some trials (1 Samuel 1:1–20). She was barren, and to make matters worse, her husband's other wife would taunt her about being childless. Hannah's husband would comfort her, but what she really wanted was a child, not just the loving concern of her husband. On one of their trips to the tabernacle, she was in deep anguish crying out to God for a son, whom she promised to give back to the Lord if He would only answer her prayers. In a somewhat humorous exchange, the high priest Eli thought Hannah was intoxicated because of how she was acting and scolded her for coming to the tabernacle drunk. After a quick explanation that she was only distressed, Eli wished her well and asked that the Lord would answer her prayers. A short time later, Hannah gave birth to Samuel in fulfillment of the requests to God.

Now came the difficult part—Hannah had to fulfill her vow to give Samuel back to God in service at the tabernacle. After she weaned him, Hannah traveled to the tabernacle and presented Samuel to Eli. Was this a difficult decision for Hannah? Maybe her mother's heart was breaking as she thought about leaving her little boy at the temple. After Hannah spent many years praying for a child, her prayer of commitment to God meant that it was time to let Samuel go. She would never get to experience his growing-up years but would instead visit him only when they came to the tabernacle. The Scriptures tell us that Hannah had five other children after Samuel, but we can be sure she felt the heartache of missing her firstborn.

In the New Testament, Jesus talks about the power of persistence in prayer. He tells many parables that bring home the singular point that God is often moved to answer our prayers because we keep asking (Matthew 7:7; Luke 18:1–8). This is Hannah's story, and it can be ours as well. There might be a prayer that we have had in our hearts for years or even decades, and we keep asking God about it while simultaneously wondering why He won't answer it. We can never pretend to understand the heart of God, but we can remember the parables about persistence in prayer and keep praying. In time, God may answer our prayer as He did with Hannah.

We all have those long-standing prayers that have remained unanswered by God. Now is the time to revisit those prayers. Write out those prayers you have been waiting on God to answer, and pray them again. Perhaps like Hannah, you would be moved to offer something to God in return for an answered prayer. While the Bible is clear that we can't manipulate God or convince Him to change His eternal purposes by our vows, it's possible that God is waiting for us to be so transformed through our prayers that we give freely of ourselves as an offering to Him.

_____

*Jesus, You know the things that I've longed
to see fulfilled in my life—would You answer
those prayers according to Your will? Amen.*

BLESSING

May you never lose hope in the God who answers
prayers. May you see the long-awaited fulfillment of
your prayers. May you, like Hannah, continue to see
more and more fruit in your life.

34

SAMUEL MISSED GOD'S VOICE

How much more do I need to say? It would take too long to recount the stories of the faith of Gideon, Barak, Samson, Jephthah, David, Samuel, and all the prophets.

HEBREWS 11:32

Dear Jesus, I don't want to miss the voice of God like Samuel did.

Meanwhile, the boy Samuel served the LORD by assisting Eli. Now in those days messages from the LORD were very rare, and visions were quite uncommon. One night Eli, who was almost blind by now, had gone to bed. The lamp of God had not yet gone out, and Samuel was sleeping in the Tabernacle near the Ark of God. Suddenly the LORD called out, "Samuel!" . . . And Samuel replied, "Speak, your servant is listening."

1 SAMUEL 3:1–4, 10

Even the prophet Samuel had to learn to listen to God. Everyone needs to start somewhere with learning to recognize the voice of God in their lives, the inner prompting that demonstrates God is speaking to us in one way or another. Samuel kept hearing the audible voice of God and mistaking it for the voice of Eli

(1 Samuel 3). Three times he went to Eli, who was just trying to sleep, and asked what Eli wanted with Samuel. The first two times, Eli told Samuel to leave him alone and go back to sleep. The third time, Eli recognized that something different was going on and advised Samuel to answer the Lord from his bed. Samuel did this, and it was then that he heard the voice of God for the moment. In Samuel's case, this was a word of judgment over Eli's house, which he had the unfortunate opportunity to share with Eli the next day.

Two things are worth noticing about this moment in Samuel's life. First, God didn't express any aggravation with Samuel for not recognizing His voice. Instead, He just waited patiently for Samuel to understand what was happening. The same is true when we are discerning how God communicates with us. In Samuel's case, God sounded a lot like Eli; for us, God might sound like our own thoughts.

The other thing worth noting about Samuel's interaction with God is that Samuel's eventual response is one of obedience: "Speak, your servant is listening." Once Samuel understood what was happening, he immediately took on a stance of receptivity to God. He didn't argue that he wasn't worthy to hear from God. After all, this same passage says that Samuel didn't even know God yet—he was imminently unqualified to hear from God (1 Samuel 3:7). No, instead, he simply replied and waited for what God would say to him. We can learn from Samuel and take a receptive stance toward God as well when it seems like He is speaking to us. Even though Samuel missed God at first, once he understood what was happening, he took the right approach.

Reading stories about the audible voice of God can feel inaccessible for us as believers. After all, who actually hears the voice of God audibly today? Not too many people. Yet we can still sense God's heartbeat for our lives as we read Scripture or pray about how to respond to a situation. Though this type of discernment is not as definitive as hearing an audible voice, there is still much we can learn about growing in prayer by paying attention to Samuel's response to God. We are still invited to make space for, and be receptive to, God's direction and guidance in our lives. The best news is that we can practice listening to God by following Samuel's example in this story. Write the following prompt: *Speak, Your servant is listening.* Then write down whatever comes to mind, if anything at all. It's been my experience that God often answers direct prayers, though obviously not always. In any case, it's a healthy practice to actively listen for God's heart in our lives.

_____

_____

_____

_____

_____

_____

_____

_____

_____

_____

_____

_____

_____

_____

_____

_____

_____

_____

_____

_____

_____

*Jesus, I long to hear Your heartbeat
for my life—speak to me, Lord, for
Your child is here listening. Amen.*

BLESSING

May you find mentors like Eli to teach you how to respond when God's heartbeat is evident in your life. May you learn to slow down and listen to what God has to say. May you continue to grow in confidence in hearing God for yourself and others.

35

NATHAN CONFRONTS DAVID'S SIN

How much more do I need to say? It would take too long to recount the stories of the faith of Gideon, Barak, Samson, Jephthah, David, Samuel, and all the prophets.

HEBREWS 11:32

Dear Jesus, I want to be courageous when You call me to something difficult, like Nathan was when You told him to confront King David.

So the LORD sent Nathan the prophet to tell David this story: "There were two men in a certain town. One was rich, and one was poor. The rich man owned a great many sheep and cattle. The poor man owned nothing but one little lamb he had bought. He raised that little lamb, and it grew up with his children. It ate from the man's own plate and drank from his cup. He cuddled it in his arms like a baby daughter. One day a guest arrived at the home of the rich man. But instead of killing an animal from his own flock or herd, he took the poor man's lamb and killed it and prepared it for his guest."

2 SAMUEL 12:1–4

Nathan had a challenging task before him. Today's narrative with Nathan the prophet follows just after David's grievous sins: those of raping Bathsheba and then killing her husband Uriah (2 Samuel 11). God tells Nathan to go to the king and confront him about his sin, and a parable about the little lamb, as featured in today's key verses, is the method God gave Nathan to confront David. This story ends with King David recognizing his sin and confessing it to God and the prophet. David has some significant consequences for his actions, but God forgives him because of his repentant heart. And it's usually David on which we focus in this story, with an emphasis on having a heart that's quick to ask for forgiveness.

Today, let's look at this story from a different perspective, that of Nathan the prophet. There is obviously no way to know what Nathan was thinking because the Bible doesn't tell us what was going on in his head. But let's take a little creative license and imagine for a moment.

Nathan was told by God to go confront the king in a dramatic way about his sin. Nathan had no idea how David was going to respond. The king could have flown into a rage and had Nathan killed. He could have imprisoned Nathan for tossing about words like *sin* and *judgment* in his earshot. Nathan had a decision to make before he ever showed up to face the king: Would he obey God or not? As we all do at one time or another (though hopefully in less stressful situations than Nathan's), he had to weigh the potential cost of obedience against choosing to ignore God and going about his day like nothing had happened.

Nathan chose obedience, but this was costly. It was obedience for which he risked his life and freedom. Nathan had been a trusted counselor of David's in the past, which means he wasn't coming to a stranger, but his association with David almost makes it worse. He potentially had relational equity to lose in the eyes of the king as well. We know that David's rage quickly dissipated as he repented in sorrow, but Nathan was living it and had no idea how it was going to turn out.

Obedience is often a scary thing for us too. Like Nathan, we don't know what the results of our obedience will be, what it will cost us, and what it will mean for our future. But still, we are called to step forward in faith, despite the unknown. Write down this question: What is God calling me to do that might have scary consequences? Answer this question as honestly as you can. If you can't think of anything right now, that's okay. In this case, think back over your life and consider a time in the past when God called you to something daunting. How did you respond, and what happened as a result? Write that down, and muse on what this might mean for you the next time God has a big request for you.

*Jesus, give me eyes to see and ears to hear
You clearly the next time You have a Nathan-
like task for me, and give me the faith to
follow through with it as he did. Amen.*

BLESSING

May you find yourself faced with a moment that requires great courage. May you rise to the challenge God gives you. May you trust God, no matter the results.

36

DANIEL SHUT THE MOUTHS OF LIONS

By faith these people overthrew kingdoms, ruled with
justice, and received what God had promised them.
They shut the mouths of lions, quenched the flames
of fire, and escaped death by the edge of the sword.
Their weakness was turned to strength. They became
strong in battle and put whole armies to flight.

HEBREWS 11:33–34

*Dear Jesus, the idea of being thrown into a lions' den is
terrifying, but You have power even over lions. I place
my trust in You in even the most terrifying situations.*

Very early the next morning, the king got up and
hurried out to the lions' den. When he got there,
he called out in anguish, "Daniel, servant of the
living God! Was your God, whom you serve so
faithfully, able to rescue you from the lions?" Daniel
answered, "Long live the king! My God sent his
angel to shut the lions' mouths so that they would
not hurt me, for I have been found innocent in his
sight. And I have not wronged you, Your Majesty."

DANIEL 6:19–22

We think we know the story of Daniel and the lions'
den. It might be one of the most familiar stories in
the Bible, so why revisit it? What can we possibly learn

that Sunday school didn't already teach us? The beauty of this story is in the buildup to the event and the immediate results that come from his survival (read the whole story in Daniel 6). Other leaders in Babylon were jealous of the Jewish adviser and captive Daniel and were trying to bring down the golden boy who was performing so well in his job. They couldn't find any dirt on him and concluded that it would only be in Daniel's worship of God that they could create problems for him. They convinced the king to pass a law decreeing that for the next thirty days, only the king should be worshiped, and then caught Daniel praying to God in his room as he did every day.

Two things stand out. First, the fact that his opponents had to create laws banning worship of God to get Daniel in trouble is a testimony to his blamelessness. There was nothing in his life that allowed for digging up any dirt at all—what a remarkable and godly leader! Second, Daniel knew the new law was passed and didn't allow it to influence his prayer time with God. As he always did, he opened his windows and prayed toward Jerusalem despite the danger involved. Daniel prioritized his devotion to God over his safety.

We know the rest of the story: Daniel was thrown into the lions' den where, to the amazement of King Darius, he survived the night! After freeing him, King Darius sent a remarkable message throughout his kingdom, which was basically the known world at the time. In this message he praised the power and authority of God, declared Him the rescuer of His people and the performer of miracles, and called God the One who will endure forever (Daniel 6:25–27). This pagan king had no choice but to acknowledge the grandeur of God and took it upon himself to share his newfound understanding of God with the known world. Who knows what the impact of such a statement from King Darius had in the world? All because Daniel lived a blameless and fearless life of faith.

There are two clear application points for us in the life of Daniel—blamelessness and fearlessness. It's time to do some heart work in relation to these concepts. Reflect on your integrity. Are you comfortable taking ethical shortcuts in your job? Do you sometimes find it easier to skirt issues of faith instead of standing your ground? Would you rather avoid talking about how your faith impacts your daily life with others? If any of these are true for you, you have some room to grow in your blamelessness. The biblical goal is to be like Daniel, where the only way to trip us up is to make belief in God illegal. Let's turn to fearlessness. Do you find it easier to back away from your faith and let it slide into the background, or are you unwilling to scale back your faith even in the face of challenges? Most of us can grow in both blamelessness and fearlessness. Reflect on how the example of Daniel and the lions' den can encourage you to grow.

_____

_____

_____

_____

_____

_____

_____

_____

_____

_____

_____

_____

*Jesus, I commit myself to serving You
wholeheartedly as Daniel did even in the
midst of a messed-up world. Amen.*

BLESSING

May you live a blameless life as Daniel did. May you be
victorious over any who seek to accuse you wrongly. May
you find your security in God alone.

37

EVEN FURNACES CAN'T BURN AWAY FAITH

By faith these people overthrew kingdoms, ruled with
justice, and received what God had promised them.
They shut the mouths of lions, quenched the flames
of fire, and escaped death by the edge of the sword.
Their weakness was turned to strength. They became
strong in battle and put whole armies to flight.

HEBREWS 11:33–34

*Dear Jesus, in those moments when hope is dim
and the odds are against me, help me to still
trust in Your character and Your goodness.*

Shadrach, Meshach, and Abednego replied, "O
Nebuchadnezzar, we do not need to defend ourselves
before you. If we are thrown into the blazing
furnace, the God whom we serve is able to save us.
He will rescue us from your power, Your Majesty.
But even if he doesn't, we want to make it clear to
you, Your Majesty, that we will never serve your
gods or worship the gold statue you have set up."

DANIEL 3:16–18

Perseverance is easier when things go our way. We
can stand firm in our faith when we know that the
outcome is in our favor. But what about the moments

when we aren't sure or when rescue seems unlikely? How do we respond then?

This is the scenario Shadrach, Meshach, and Abednego faced in Daniel 3; one where calamity was almost guaranteed. Nebuchadnezzar had created a ninety-foot-tall gold statue of himself and demanded everyone to bow and worship this statue or be thrown into a furnace of fire. Shadrach, Meshach, and Abednego refused, even after being given a second chance in front of the king to worship. Enraged, King Nebuchadnezzar threatened again to throw them into the furnace; today's key verses from the book of Daniel records their response. In these verses, you can see that they have a calm assurance that God could rescue them, but they will continue to serve Him even if He doesn't. Because they were not willing to bow down to anyone but God, the three Hebrews were thrown into the furnace and were rescued by an angel. The king saw not three but four men walking around in the fire and called them out, astonished at the grandeur of God and His power. The king even issued a proclamation that nobody could bad-mouth the Lord under the penalty of death (Daniel 3:28–29).

There will be seasons in our lives when we can be nearly certain that bad things are coming. A late-stage cancer diagnosis comes to mind, where God could bring restoration, but the odds are that He won't. These are the toughest times, when it's easy to allow questioning of God's goodness to seep into our bones. If God can heal, why won't He? What could He be looking to accomplish in this terrible event? The truth is that we will likely never get an answer to those questions. During times when nothing makes sense, we must learn to trust God in the dark. Let's be honest—any explanation God could give would likely be unhelpful anyway, because we would be focused on our pain. But there is space for us to trust the character of God even in such trials, as Shadrach, Meshach, and Abednego did all those years ago.

Trusting God when all is dark isn't easy. No matter how long we've walked with God, imminent bad news can rock our faith if we let it. We can be shipwrecked by a terrible turn of events in our lives and never recover because we feel God is untrustworthy. At the same time, we can choose in those moments to recall the goodness God has shown us during the rest of our history with Him.

Remembering God's faithfulness to us when we are in a season of trial can be incredibly challenging, but faith can survive terrible events. The best way to prepare for this is to have a record of the ways God has proven Himself faithful. Let's start that process now. Write down how God has answered a prayer of yours or shown His love for you in a remarkable way. Be as detailed as possible because you will need this record later. The truth is that we are always coming out of a tragedy, waiting for a tragedy, or entering a new one, because this world is broken. We have to be prepared for dark times, and having a record of God's faithfulness is a great way to prepare our faith for difficult times.

*Jesus, stir greater faith in my soul as I
relive those moments when You've proven
Your love to me in the past. Amen.*

BLESSING

May you develop a steadfast love for God through dark times. May your faith survive the next tragedy because you've remembered His goodness. May your perseverance last.

38

THE SHUNAMMITE WOMAN'S FAITH

Women received their loved ones
back again from death.

HEBREWS 11:35

Dear Jesus, even in the darkest moments of my life, give
me the strength to push through to the unbelievable,
instead of accepting sorrow as my lot in life.

When Elisha arrived, the child was indeed dead, lying
there on the prophet's bed. He went in alone and shut
the door behind him and prayed to the LORD. . . . Elisha
got up, walked back and forth across the room once,
and then stretched himself out again on the child. This
time the boy sneezed seven times and opened his eyes!

2 KINGS 4:32–33, 35

Ho-hum, Elisha raised a dead child from the grave.
The miracle in this story is told in a very matter-of-fact
way, as though there was nothing special about the event.
Perhaps for this extraordinary prophet, this really wasn't a
remarkable event, though it certainly seems amazing from
our perspective. Let's focus on the child's mom and her
actions, the one known as the "woman of Shunem" or the
"Shunammite woman" (read the Shunammite woman's
story in 2 Kings 4:8–37). This child was given to her in

her husband's old age as a surprise gift of sorts from God, and she cherished the boy deeply. He suddenly fell ill and died nearly instantly with no reason given in the text, but she never lost hope.

Immediately this Shunammite woman went about the work of finding a miracle. She saddled a donkey and rode hard to find Elisha. When she found him, she appealed to his emotions and convinced him to return with her. This is where today's verses from 2 Kings pick up the story. Upon arriving at her home, Elisha laid on top of the child twice and resuscitated him. Then the woman of Shunem bowed in overwhelming gratitude at Elisha's feet and carried her son downstairs. Even in her darkest night, the Shunammite woman trusted that God, through Elisha, could do the impossible

It can be dangerous to presume a miracle is coming as this woman did, and it's worth talking about for a moment here. We must be certain that God's blessing is on the miracle, or we will end up wasting our energy pursuing something God never intended. But when God is in something, we should chase it with all the energy and passion that we see in this determined mother. Even in the darkest of nights, there is a place for seeking a miracle. Let's not allow ourselves to forget that we serve the Creator of the universe and that He loves us more deeply than we can understand. Who knows what God's plan is in the midst of the darkest night?

Many of us have experienced that darkest-night moment where our world just starts falling apart. Maybe it's a sudden job loss when you loved your company. Perhaps it's an

unexpected death in the family. The world has trained us to just take it and try to move forward, but the Shunammite woman shows us that we can do something different—we can plead with God for things to change . . . and they just might because God loves us desperately. There is power available to us when we sit in our dissatisfaction with our situation and use that dissatisfaction to push us to prayer and holy intervention. Reflect on a time when you didn't want to accept the terrible thing that was happening in your life. What did you do to fight against the despair or the anger that you felt? Did God refresh the circumstances so that tragedy was turned into triumph? How else did God show Himself present in the midst of your tragedy? Even if God didn't rescind the terrible event, how was He there? It's important to remember His presence in your sorrow, so focus on His activity in the midst of your despair and frustration. God promises that we will never be left as orphans in this world. Even though it might feel like we are alone sometimes, our Father is always by our side.

Jesus, show me the balance between not accepting a terrible fate and recognizing Your presence in the midst of dark seasons. Amen.

BLESSING

May you find tenacity when things are starting to fall apart. May you pursue God with everything you've got, holding fast in faith that God can make a change in your life. May you know when to accept the dark times and look for the tender presence of God anyway.

39

NO INDIVIDUALIZED PERFECTION

All these people earned a good reputation
because of their faith, yet none of them
received all that God had promised.

HEBREWS 11:39

*Dear Jesus, remind me that Christianity is not a solo
sport and that it's only possible to achieve all that
God has for me in community with other believers.*

Let us hold tightly without wavering to the hope
we affirm, for God can be trusted to keep his
promise. Let us think of ways to motivate one
another to acts of love and good works. And
let us not neglect our meeting together, as some
people do, but encourage one another, especially
now that the day of his return is drawing near.

HEBREWS 10:23–25

We've spent a lot of time looking at heroes of the
faith in this book. The remarkable thing is that
none of them received everything God promised. Abraham never saw the land of Canaan become his inheritance, and neither did Sarah. David never saw the temple
built in his lifetime. The list goes on, and this is a powerful
truth for us to consider carefully. It means that we are

never able to accomplish the fullness of what God has for us if we act alone. Faith is not a singular enterprise—it always involves a group of people moving together. Even when Abraham was first called by God as the father of many nations, Sarah was right by his side. Abraham was not alone. But there's a deeper truth here—none of us can fully satisfy God's best for our lives in isolation. This is why Hebrews 11:39 says each person didn't receive all that God had promised them, because God was looking to invest in all those who desired to love and follow Him. He still is today.

Life gets hard sometimes, and we lose heart. When we lose heart, we can easily stop all the acts of love and good works that God desires us to demonstrate in our lives. Add to it the fact that sometimes we don't want to be involved in the body of Christ, and we end up isolated and unmotivated. This is where a community has all its power. It is in community with other believers that we can be encouraged to keep up the good work of demonstrating the kindness of our great God in this dark world. When we find ourselves discouraged or facing a tough season of life, others can come alongside us and strengthen us so we don't despair.

It's time for another heart check. How focused are you on being in community with other believers? Consider this statement: I can't accomplish God's best for me without other believers. Do you believe that statement to be true, and does your life reflect this belief? If your answer to either part of that question is no, it's never too late to start investing in community. You can always begin the hard work of finding your tribe, your safe community, that space where you know you are heard, loved, and accepted. Start today with a commitment to never stop looking for that community until you find it.

_____

_____

_____

_____

_____

_____

_____

_____

_____

_____

_____

_____

_____

*Jesus, don't let me settle for an
individualistic faith but drive me into
community with others. Amen.*

BLESSING

May you find your trustworthy tribe. May you be spurred on to good deeds. May you invest intentionally in other people's lives so that their faith in Christ can grow too.

40

JESUS OUR CHAMPION

Therefore, since we are surrounded by such a huge
crowd of witnesses to the life of faith, let us strip off
every weight that slows us down, especially the sin that
so easily trips us up. And let us run with endurance
the race God has set before us. We do this by keeping
our eyes on Jesus, the champion who initiates and
perfects our faith. Because of the joy awaiting him,
he endured the cross, disregarding its shame. Now he
is seated in the place of honor beside God's throne.
Think of all the hostility he endured from sinful
people; then you won't become weary and give up.

HEBREWS 12:1–3

*Dear Jesus, You are my champion, and I love
You. Thank You for enduring the shame of
the cross to initiate my faith, and thank You
for perfecting my faith every day since.*

What if these heroes of the faith are literally cheering us on in the heavenly realms (Hebrews 12:1)?
Whenever we feel utterly alone, we can find strength in
this idea—Abraham and Moses and Jochebed and Rahab
and Sarah and many others are almost certainly watch-
ing and encouraging us to keep going even when times
get rough. And we know that other believers in our lives
who have passed on are cheering for us. This is especially
encouraging when we find ourselves caught in a sinful

pattern. Sin can powerfully entrap us when we're not paying attention, and before we know it, we find ourselves stuck. In these moments, we can borrow strength from the heroes of the past or those around us today.

We can also recall how these heroes struggled at times to make the right choices yet God still used them. We can take courage in this idea that God doesn't need perfect people. Moses killed an Egyptian, and it cost him forty years in the wilderness. Abraham lied twice about whether Sarah was his wife, and a plague fell upon the people he was visiting. Jacob was a schemer his whole life, but he is one of the patriarchs and the whole nation is called by his new name, Israel. Gideon allowed fear to reign in his life in a variety of different ways before he finally settled on obedience, and Barak let his fear prevent him from being fully obedient. Yet God used all these people despite these shortcomings and sins; surely God has a plan for our lives too.

Beyond looking to the heroes of the faith or those around us, we can look to the example of Jesus. He endured the worst possible torture of dying on a cross and being separated for a season from the love and acceptance of His heavenly Father, but He never gave up. How was He able to accomplish something this tremendous? Jesus endured suffering "for the joy set before him" (Hebrews 12:2 NIV). While we obviously aren't God like Jesus, we can do the same when we are walking through the valley of the shadow of death. We can remind ourselves that our current struggles are nothing compared to the glory that is to be revealed in us (Romans 8:18), and we can be encouraged by God's grand goodness displayed toward us.

It's time for your last entry. Consider afresh the scorn that Jesus endured to bring us back into a relationship with God the Father, and allow praise and gratitude for God's love for you to rise up in your spirit. Write down the first thoughts that come to your mind when you think of the cross. It could be a worship song that you really enjoy, or maybe it's a snippet from a recent sermon. It doesn't have to be anything original or remarkable; just write down the first things you think of. Allow yourself to feel gratitude toward God and to praise Him for a moment longer. Write down a prayer of thanksgiving to Jesus for all He went through to restore our relationship with God.

_____

_____

_____

_____

_____

_____

_____

_____

_____

_____

_____

_____

_____

_____

Jesus, You're the best. Thank You for
paving the way for me to draw close to God
through Your sacrifice on the cross. Amen.

BLESSING

May you always find encouragement in the crowd of
witnesses cheering you on in your faith walk. May you
never grow weary of considering Jesus and the cross.
May you forever find hope in His sacrifice.

ACKNOWLEDGMENTS

First and foremost, I need to thank my family. You put up with me fixating over every word that I typed in this manuscript and the near-constant questioning of whether my heart would come out on the pages with a particular vocabulary choice. You tolerated my being not present even when I was home and working at my desk for months on end with my noise-canceling headphones on, just asking nonverbally to be left alone. Through it all, you encouraged me and challenged me to keep going. Barbara, Cynthia, Elijah, and Ellen—thanks for believing in me and giving me space to create this book.

A million thanks go to Mary DeMuth. You believed in me before most did by speaking truth and power into my life through conference classes and masterminds and podcasts. I appreciate you more than words can say, and I was overwhelmed with enthusiasm and joy to finally meet you in person after having been influenced by you for so many years. Thanks as well to everyone at Books & Such Literary Agency for seeing a book worth publishing in this proposal. A special thank you to Janet Grant for seeing this project through to its completion.

I'm grateful to the entire team at Our Daily Bread Publishing. Thanks for seeing a devotional worth investing in. Thank you for the time and effort you put into capturing the very best of my words.

Finally, thanks to God for plopping this idea in my head one afternoon during my Bible study. You are a truly amazing, creative God and I'm grateful for you.

Spread the Word
by Doing One Thing.

- Give a copy of this book as a gift.
- Share the QR code link via your social media.
- Write a review of this book on your blog, favorite bookseller's website, or at ODB.org/store.
- Recommend this book to your church, small group, or book club.

Connect with us. [f] [○] 🕊

Our Daily Bread Publishing
PO Box 3566, Grand Rapids, MI 49501, USA
Email: books@odb.org

Love God. Love Others.

with  Our Daily Bread.

Your gift changes lives.

Connect with us. 🅕 ⊡ 🐦

Our Daily Bread Publishing
PO Box 3566, Grand Rapids, MI 49501, USA
Email: books@odb.org

How do you deepen your relationship with and understanding of God?

At the source.
Get to know Him through His own Word, the Bible.

Know Him devotes 365 days to revealing the character of God solely through Scripture. These passages, drawn from every book of the Bible, highlight twelve unchanging attributes of our Creator. Whether you're new to the Bible or a longtime reader, you'll gain a deeper awe of God's holiness, transcendence, and glory along with a renewed appreciation for His mercy, justice, and truth.

Buy It Today